CHALLENGES
OF THE
CROOKED
PATH

SHIRLEY J. GILBERT, PH.D

Printed in the United States of America
ISBN: Softcover   978-1-63871-698-3
             eBook   978-1-63871-699-0
Republished by: PageTurner Press and Media LLC
Publication Date: 11/05/2021

To order copies of this book, contact:
PageTurner Press and Media
Phone: 1-888-447-9651
info@pageturner.us
www.pageturner.us

CHALLENGES
OF THE
CROOKED
PATH

SHIRLEY J GILBERT
WOODSIDE, CA 2021

Contents

Introduction

The conclusions of this four-book series tell a story of immense challenges for Andy and his family.

The crooked path can present enormous challenges that can move us to ecstasy or break our hearts. Every main character in the stories of the crooked path have endured severe challenges.

From Sam's boyhood to Andy's final years, there is a continuing saga of events throughout the stories of the crooked path, many of which are almost unbelievable.

For each of us, the path presents challenges we often don't foresee. Some of them break our hearts. The strength that humans endure to keep going is beyond belief, especially for Andy.

This final story of Andy's life, while tragic, is linked to reality for most of us. We often endure challenges that look like mountains we are unprepared to climb. We find we get to the top just one step at a time. We finally come to understand and accept that the challenges of the complex and crooked path will always be there.

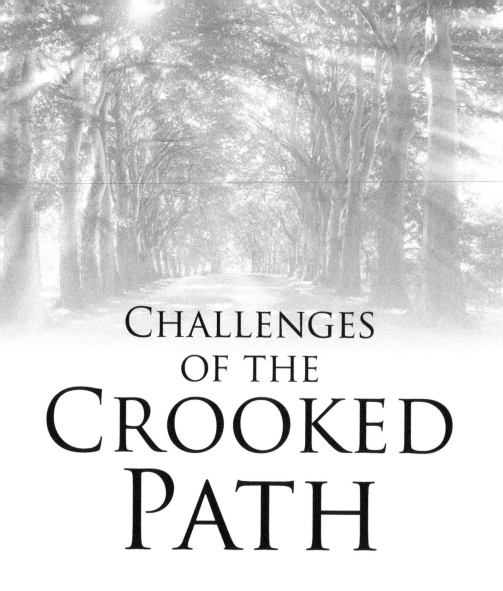

CHALLENGES
OF THE
CROOKED
PATH

Chapter One

Saving Joey

Now that the Clinic, the sister facility of the Arthur Gates Foundation, was up and running, he was very grateful for what seemed to be a calm season of his life.

He and Kristy have never been closer. The children seemed to be thriving. Kristy's cancer was gone. Andy spent time sitting in his favorite chair, looking out to the ocean and wondered what kinds of challenges were down the road.

Today, he and Champion were headed down the beach for a run. Andy was making it a point to pay attention to taking care of himself. Besides, it was a beautiful day.

Andy tried to use his workouts productively. He used it as a time to think about what he could or needed to do to reach out to others. That day, he was thinking about Mary up in Seattle who had made it her mission in life to take care of stray dogs.

Andy had a mountain of respect for her. It was important to him to continue to try to support her both personally as well as financially. In fact, he made it a point to remember that he should call her as soon as he got back home. She has such a heart for helping animals. He really saw her as one of the unseen angels in the world. She has a heart of gold.

Just as he and Champion were crossing a busy street, he looked over and was aware of a small child heading into traffic by himself. There didn't appear to be anyone with him. Andy raced to the child and picked him up as he was about to go straight into oncoming traffic. Horns were honking.

"Hey there, buddy. Where's your Mommy?" Andy asked.

The little guy started to cry. Andy got him out of harm's way and out of the bright sunshine. He looked around again to see if there was an adult anywhere who was looking after him. He didn't see anyone.

Andy spent the next 20 minutes talking with, trying to comfort and get some information about the child. Finally, he decided he needed to call 911 and get the authorities involved.

It took them less than ten minutes to arrive.

Andy gave the female officer as much information as he knew (which was very little) and turned the child over to her. He left his name, address and phone number. He inquired if he could get her card and inquire of the child's condition later in the day.

Andy and Champion jogged back to their house. Andy couldn't imagine how he could have found that little guy all by himself. He just kept saying, "Mommy, mommy, mommy" and screaming. It was very upsetting for Andy. He was very familiar with child trauma. The only other thing the child said was,

"Me--Joey."

When Andy arrived home, the children were just coming home from school. It was their time to talk about the events of the day. Little Dan had fallen down that day on the playground and had a bandaid on his scraped knee. Alice got an A on her spelling test and little Alana had survived another day at preschool.

Kristy had met a new neighbor and was eager to share with Andy all about her and her family. They had children about the same age as their children. They were both excited about it. All of this got his mind off the child he had found earlier.

After dinner, the news was on the television. Front and center was a story about a woman they had found murdered that day on the beach. She was young and there were several child's toys near where they found her. They were requesting help from the public to identify her. They didn't say how she died.

Andy found the card the officer had given him that day. He called the number and asked for her. She was not available but Andy left his number and requested a call back.

It was 9 PM when Andy's cell phone rang. It was the officer who had taken custody of the child. Andy told her he had learned of the murdered woman they had found on the beach and wondered if she could be the mother of the child he had found. He also inquired as to the whereabouts of the child.

The officer explained that the child had been turned over to Child Family Services. They had not had any reports of a missing child from anyone. They were totally uncertain why he was wandering in traffic.

Andy felt very concerned for the child. He mentioned to the officer that he and his family lived nearby. For some reason, he also mentioned that he was from Seattle, had been the CEO of the Arthur Gates Foundation and had established a Clinic here in the Bay area.

There was a long pause. Andy asked if the officer was still on the line. She mentioned to him that they had found a card among the murdered woman's belongings that was from the Clinic he had described.

Andy asked whose name was on the card. He was shocked when she told him. It was one of the therapists he had hired.

Andy asked if there was any more information she could share. Would a picture be available or could he at least describe her -- height, weight, hair color, age, etc.

She suggested, as a last resort, that he and the woman whose name was on the card could view the body in hopes of identifying her. There were no identifying documents with her when they found her. Someone had noticed the blood soaked towel she was lying on. She had apparently been stabbed.

Andy asked if he could call her back to book a time for them to come. He said he would need to contact the therapist first.

She agreed that would be fine.

Although it was late by this time, Andy contacted the therapist. He explained to her the circumstances and asked if she might have some time tomorrow to make a trip to the morgue with him.

Before they hung up, they had agreed on a time. Andy would drive his car, come by the Clinic and they would go together. Somehow, he wasn't looking forward to it but believed it was the right thing to do.

Before turning out the light, Andy shared with Allison what had happened that day and what he had agreed to do the next day. Kristy was very sympathetic and praised him for helping the child.

Precisely at 2 PM the next day, Andy picked up Joyce, the therapist whose card the woman had in her possession. They found it in the back of the child's stroller at the beach. They made their way to the morgue.

Joyce was running through her head the patients she was treating there at the Clinic. She could think of two who had a young son. One of them was a case of severe domestic violence.

When they arrived at the morgue, the officer was waiting for them. Andy introduced Joyce to the officer. The officer asked them to follow her. They went into the bowels of the large building to a remote area. She simply nodded to the orderly standing by.

He apparently was aware of why they were there. They brought out the body and slowly removed the sheet from her face.

Joyce's hand went over her face. She recognized her immediately. It was Karen. She had seen her at least three times. She was terrified of her ex-husband. She had a restraining order against him. She had received several death threats from him. The police had been called multiple times.

Unbeknown to anyone, that day at the beach, Karen had spotted her ex-husband and ran down the beach with her son in her arms. She bought him an ice-cream cone and made him promise to stay there until she came back for him. He said, "Okay, Mommy," and smiled at her. She never returned.

Once again, Andy's compassionate heart motivated him to grab little Joey and save him from oncoming traffic. There were plenty of others who could have done it that day, but they didn't. It is clear to all of us by now that Andy is, in fact, a doer, an unseen angel.

Andy is working to integrate his outside interests with the balance of his beautiful family. He is ever more aware since his airplane accident and memory loss. He nearly lost everything. He has been a changed man since then.

Andy appears to do very well with helping others and then finding ways to bring that person into balance with his own goals. For such a busy man he seems to find very creative ways to make that happen.

For example, after Andy discovered that Joeys' mother had been murdered and that there was no father listed on the birth certificate, he had Joey removed to the Foundation to care for him. That was an ingenious move plus it gives Andy the opportunity both to bond with and form some kind of relationship with him over time.

Joey's mother was a client at the Clinic which also caused Andy to feel some responsibility for him. He found ways to make several important linkages, all to ensure Joey's care and well being. Andy follows through. He is a God-send to many different people besides Joey. It simply is who he is.

Chapter Two

Life and Death Challenges

By the time they left the morgue, Joyce was in tears.

She could remember vividly her session with Karen two days ago. She was terrified and extremely protective of her son.

Joyce had tried to be as supportive as possible by telling her she had alerted the police, filed a restraining order and that she needed to try to have as normal a life as possible and enjoy her son. That is likely why she was on the beach that day, trying to enjoy her life and her son.

Joyce and Andy were both distraught. The people they were treating at the Clinic were very different from treating children at the Foundation.

Private practice included every known problem known to mankind. Also, there simply wasn't the protection that the Foundation provided. Andy actually had no experience whatsoever with these kinds of issues.

Because Andy is who he is, he felt compelled to follow up on this case. He was beyond angry at men who hurt/murder women, especially those with small children. Because he was basically the one in charge of the Clinics and because Karen had sought help there, Andy decided to do his best to follow up on this case.

Andy contacted the officer once more and made an appointment to meet with her Captain. He explained that he was the one who had found the child and that the child's mother had been seeking treatment at a Clinic he supervised.

The Captain pulled the file and confirmed there had, in fact, been a number of times she had called to report domestic violence. Her husband always managed to find a way to avoid any jail time. The statement in the file said directly, "He is going to kill me." Apparently, she was right.

Andy saw the name of Karen's husband from the file as it lay open on the desk. He knew just the person to contact to check it out. He would call Ralph that night.

In the meantime, he wanted to follow up on Karen. He wondered if her parents were alive, if she had any siblings, etc. He wanted to know what he could do to help. It was simply who he was.

He learned that Karen's father was serving time in prison and that her mother had died when she was young. She did have a younger sister. Andy might pay her a visit if he could locate her.

Andy contacted Ralph that evening and explained the circumstances of Karen's case to him. He inquired if Ralph could give him a week of his time to help him. He told him that he would cover all of his expenses and make it worth his while.

They made arrangements for Ralph to meet with Andy at 4 PM. He asked specifically if he could track down the sister and the ex-husband.

By the end of the week, Ralph had addresses for Andy of both the sister and the ex-husband. He had done some surveillance of each of them and reported his findings.

Karen's sister hung out mostly in bars, appeared to be single and wasn't home much. She had a small apartment in a bad section of town. Apparently, she didn't have a steady job.

The ex-husband lived in a very upscale part of town. He hung out at a gentlemen's club, drove an expensive car and flashed a lot of cash in public. He ran with a fast crowd with lots of money and power. He dressed well and presented himself as an important and upstanding citizen. Ralph had noticed a number of women coming and going from his residence at all hours.

Andy surmised that Karen had a rough childhood and had gotten involved with a man who didn't want a child. He was determined not to have to support him. He likely paid someone to remove her from his life, from everyone's life.

Ralph inquired if there was a way to obtain DNA from the man to determine if he was, in fact, the baby's father and find a way for him to have to support his son. Ralph said he would give it his best shot.

By the end of the week, he produced an empty bottle of water with the man's DNA on it. He had fished it out of a public trash can, but was certain it was his.

Andy decided to get back to the captain at the police station, get a DNA sample from the child, provide the DNA on the empty bottle of water and see if there was a match. If so, the man could be made to provide financially for little Joey's needs.

Joey's DNA and that found on the water bottle was a perfect match.

As Andy thought about that precious child he had rescued from traffic, he couldn't help but think of the three detectives his grandfather had hired to track down Hiram and find a way to destroy him.

He realized this would be a very extreme and expensive way to handle this situation, but he could afford it and was very tempted to make it happen. Little Joey deserved better than a dead mother and a father who wished he'd never been born.

Andy decided to hold that thought. He would find a way to observe the man himself and then decide whether he needed to drop the whole issue, or pursue it.

Andy convinced Ralpy to stay through the week-end and to lead him to a place where he could, personally, observe this loser. Ralph pulled a few strings and got them into the Gentlemen's Club for dinner. They made certain they dressed the part. They would present themselves as stock market executives. They would wear flashy Rolex watches, lots of gold, and flash significant cash and make it a point to catch this guy's attention. It worked. His name was Brad.

Andy introduced him and Ralph as a couple of stock market gurus from Seattle. He smiled and offered to buy them drinks, which they accepted.

Over the next hour, they bantered with small talk about irrelevant things. They listened carefully to Brad's pitch about his royal lifestyle, bankroll and access to everything. He had his script perfected to Hollywood standards. He told them he could get them any girl they wanted. He could do it all, including drugs. Whatever they wanted was in his grasp. Just name it!

Andy and Ralph left the Club around midnight. They both felt very clear about who Brad was. This was going to require a very complex approach. In fact, Andy and Ralph spent the next few hours discussing all of the possibilities for handling this guy. It actually reminded Andy of their discussion many years ago about how to handle Hiram. That turned out to be ingenious.

One of the ideas that crossed Ralph's mind was to call upon a female detective they sometimes used to help them. In fact, he flatly suggested he thought this would be the way to go. At least, it was probably the best way to start the process and see how Brad responds.

Andy is an unusual man. He has a stellar belief in justice.

He also had the means to ensure it when his tenacious self decided to make it happen. He had done it many times before and it has almost become part of his modus operandi.

Andy is a champion of childhood healing. He has lived it.

He has led the Foundation which embodies the mission of helping traumatized children. Little Joey fits into that category.

Perhaps because of Andy's own private history, he has a heightened sensitivity to issues of right and wrong, good and bad, justice and lawlessness. It is always very clear which side he is on. His tenacity provides him drive and strength to problem solve on the side of goodness. It almost seems to be hardwired into his DNA.

Finding ways to get people to take responsibility for their behaviors requires great energy and ingenuity. Andy has both. With the help of Ralph and his associates, he has found the help he needs to do his work. This is thanks, in part, to his incredible grandfather. In spite of all of the trauma in Andy's life, he has been given several incredible gifts which have formed his crooked path.

Andy's growing affection for little Joey and his absolute disdain for his father is directing his efforts in ways he believes will get his attention and send his life in a different direction.

Chapter Three

Retribution for Joey

The next call Andy made was to the Foundation.

He spoke with the CEO and explained the circumstances about little Joey. He inquired as to the possibility of getting Joey into the program there. He thought he would be most appropriate and explained his reasons.

Andy was told they would get back to him regarding their question. There was a very complex procedure and backlog for potential residents there at the Foundation. He would do a thorough investigation and get back with him shortly.

In the meantime, Andy contacted the Captain at the police station, reported his findings and told him about the Foundation. He asked what the procedure would be to transfer young Joey out of foster care into the Foundation.

There existed no paternal listing on little Joey's birth certificate which made the entire process easier. Through the efforts of several unseen angels, all of the pieces came together for the transfer to be handled. Andy was delighted. He believed it was no accident that he had been the one who spotted little Joey in dangerous traffic. The timing of all of it had not been coincidental. Andy believed in signs. He had certainly experienced enough of them in his own life.

Once Joey was safely transferred, Andy contacted his three detective friends who were actually residents of that area. He continued to talk with Ralph, the lead detective, briefed him about the current events and made plans for the four of them to meet.

Andy gave Ralph an update about Brad. Ralph suggested that the three of them be given the opportunity to spend some time with him and make their assessment. Andy agreed.

The next two weeks, Ralph was a frequent guest at the Gentlemen's Club. He knew exactly how to fit right in and eventually find his way to Brad. He worked to gain his trust. One night, as Ralph continued to buy Brad drinks, he heard a little about a woman who "was no longer around" who learned not to cross him. He made it clear that he was not a man to be crossed. There were dire consequences for anyone who did that. He laughed and said, "I could give you a list of their sorry asses."

Andy and Ralph meet again. Ralph explained his impressions of Brad. He could actually think of several creative ways to get at this guy. He wanted to know just how serious Andy wanted to be about punishing this guy.

Andy liked Ralph's idea of bringing in one of his female colleagues who "had a body that wouldn't quit." He was sure Brad would take the bait. The more Ralph talked, the more Andy liked it. Basically, Ralph would be handing the baton off to Sheila.

She was about as street smart, seductive and punishing as any woman he knew. Andy liked it. He thought it was exactly what he deserved. Let the games begin.

Andy really didn't want to know any part of what Sheila and Ralph were planning. He just wanted to be informed of the results. It wouldn' take very long before there were results.

Brad first observed Sheila at the Club. He couldn't take his eyes off of her. He found a way to approach her and asked if he could buy her a drink. She brushed him off seductively. He continued to pursue her to the point where he felt she was doing him a favor to let him have a drink with her. It was all falling into place.

Once Sheila had his attention, she began to work her magic on him. He was totally into it, totally into her. Unbeknown to him, drugs were put in his drink that was used to make large animals mate. He was desperate. He offered her $10,000 for one quick roll in the hay. His room was less than one minute away. They scurried off. He was in pain and they hadn't even gotten to the room yet. It was over before it had hardly begun. She made certain he believed it was the best sex he ever had in his life. She left the room, with his $10,000.

Sheila made it a point not to show up at Brad's Club again for at least two weeks. When she came through the door, looking like a million dollars, he practically broke his neck getting to her.

She hardly noticed him and let him know it. He was begging for some action. She smiled and moved away. Unbeknown to Brad, Sheila had brought along a fellow detective to help her play the game. She was showing erotic attention to him which was driving Brad mad.

Brad finally approached her, grabbed her arm, and said he had to see her. She smiled, touched his face and said, "I'm with someone." He stood there looking pathetic.

Sheila and her fellow detective stayed for about an hour in a corner booth, all over each other. Brad was seething with desire and jealousy.

Brad watched them leave together, followed them outside and took notice of the car they drove. He got the license plate and had every intention of getting the information he wanted. He would have his way, no matter what!

Sheila and her fellow detective were smart enough not to use their actual license plate. It belonged to a fellow detective. It was his car. They were eager to see what lengths Brad would sink and were prepared for whatever they were.

Sure enough, one night later, Brad himself came through an unlocked window into the apartment. He had climbed the fire escape, very determined to make entry. As he closed the window, once inside, he made his way into the bedroom. There he believed he saw Sheila, naked in the bed, sound asleep.

Brad could hardly get his clothes off fast enough. Just as he finished getting naked, all of the lights came on, the woman in the bed was a mannequin. He was carrying a gun. 911 was called and he was immediately placed under arrest for breaking, entering, sexual assault and carrying a weapon.

His troubles were just beginning!

In a call the next morning, Andy was given all of the details of the events from the night before. Brad was in jail, awaiting charges for breaking, entering, sexual intent, and carrying a weapon. Ralph also had intentions of scouring his financial dealings. Those charges were undetermined as of yet.

Andy began to think about the whole issue of karma. It seemed to him that life has many ways of dealing with each of us, depending on our behavior and the way we live our lives.

Sometimes it seems as though evil and lawlessness doesn't seem to have many consequences. However, we don't really know what is going on behind the scenes or in people's hearts and minds. Andy needed to believe that, in fact, there is karma for everyone, whether it's obvious to the rest of us or not.

Andy is troubled by the connection between little Joey and his father. Somehow, he wants to make certain there cannot be any claims down the road between the two of them. Paternity would be a very convincing factor in a court of law. Andy would never want Joey to have much to do with a man like Brad.

As he had done all of his life, Andy knew he simply had to cast his bread on the water and trust the process. Although he hadn't always liked or appreciated the results, he believed them to be the way life was supposed to be. After all, he was not in charge of the Universe.

Chapter Four

Brad's Crooked Path

Brad already had a police record for domestic violence, violating a restraining order and a person of interest in his wife's death. Now he had additional charges which were not going to be dismissed so easily. They included breaking, entering, suggestion of rape and carrying a weapon. He was going down.

Andy was delighted. They had now used up their plan for Sheila. It was time to move to stage two. It was time to go after his finances. Research would be conducted which would reveal his specific sources of income, any tax evasion or undeclared income. They had access to tax attorneys who could scrutinize his records in a short time and reveal any shortcomings.

Andy and the detectives were enjoying this process. Somehow they felt as though they were part of some kind of karma followup for people like Brad. Maybe they were some part of supplying justice for a dead mother and abandoned child.

Brad's bail was a million dollars. His passport was taken and he wore an ankle bracelet. The humiliation for him was worth the entire effort. He didn't dare inhabit the Gentlemen's Club wearing an ankle bracelet. His buddies wondered what happened to him.

The tax attorney was able to come up with tax evasion issues totalling nearly ten million dollars. This, added to his pending sentence, was not looking good for him. He was looking at a decade behind bars.

At that point, Brad said he had some information regarding a murder and he would reveal it if it would reduce his sentence. The District Attorney asked him, "And just what information would that be?"

Brad said he had a group of very good friends. One of them was very upset because his wife wanted Brad to pay child support. If he had to do that, it would take away from the money Brad was giving him each month for drugs, so he killed her. He stabbed her through the heart on a beach in San Francisco. He gave the man's name, said he saw him do it and would testify in court.

The process that followed took months. The man Brad identified as the one who murdered his wife said Brad paid him $200,000 to kill her. He was the one who instigated the murder.

Over a period of many months, the man was put on trial and convicted of Karen's murder. Brad testified he witnessed it there on the beach.

Although the man was convicted for his wife's murder, the judge believed the guilty man when he said he was paid to do it. Andy, Sheila and Ralph were all present in the courtroom when Brad was sentenced. The judge gave him the maximum sentence of eight years in prison. It wasn't the death sentence he should have had for killing his wife and abandoning his son, but it was a start.

Both men left the courtroom in handcuffs, escorted to prison. They even rode in the same van on their way to the same prison.

As they were exiting the van, the man convicted of Karen's murder grabbed a deputy's gun and shot Brad in the face before he could be restrained. The bullet went through his brain and rendered him brain dead for the rest of his life. His body survived. For all practical purposes, his life was over.

Andy read about the incident in the next day's newspaper.

He realized that had he not pursued Brad initially, this would never have happened to him. He realized he had strong instincts about bringing him to justice . He believed karma had done its job. He had no regrets.

In the meantime, Andy was sorry that Joey didn't have a father in his life. Under the circumstances, he believed he was probably better off being raised at the Foundation.

Andy was following little Joey's development at the Foundation. He was doing very well. In fact, Andy was headed back to Seattle to meet with the Board of Directors regarding the Clinic. He would be able to see him then. Perhaps he could establish some kind of meaningful connection with him. Maybe he could even be his unseen angel. Maybe he already was.

After dinner that night, Andy was sitting in his favorite chair, looking out at the ocean. His dog, Champion, was beside him and his wife and children were in the house. He felt overwhelmed with God's blessings in his life. Andy had what seemed like a million memories of his past, made up of high highs and low lows.

As Andy reflected on the events that had occurred since he pulled little Joey out of oncoming traffic, he spent time reflecting on many events in his life.

From the time Andy was a small child, his entire life has been filled with many unforeseen challenges on his crooked path. Although he felt he had little understanding of why that was, he somehow always had the feeling that he was being guided by some unforeseen force.

Andy felt as though he was always given the strength and insight to go in the direction he felt led to go. It was only afterward that he understood that. There were times he just wanted to quit, to be done with trying to help anyone do anything. He longed for someone to help him. He would always cherish the memory of his grandfather who was the one person in his life who came to his rescue at the most critical point in his life.

Speaking of karma, what if Andy didn't have a grandfather?

Who, where, how would he be now? Although we each have choices on our crooked path, we don't seem to be in charge of who or what crosses our path. That is such a critical piece of our entire journey.

This reality has never been more clear to Andy.

Chapter Five

Challenges at the Farm

Just then, Andy's cell phone rang. It was Mary from Seattle. She said there had been a bad fire at the farm the night before. It had done considerable damage. Fortunately, she didn't lose any animals, but nearly half of their kennels had been destroyed and the dogs were upset. They were the ones who woke her up and alerted her to the fire.

The fire marshal believed the fire was arson. There was a long pause. Andy could hardly believe what he was hearing.

Who would want to destroy such a beautiful place where homeless dogs found shelter and love?

Andy told Mary he would make arrangements to come to the farm by the end of the week. He would let her know when he would be there. He expressed his sympathy and said he would be in touch.

Andy told Kristy what was happening with Mary and that he was thinking of heading to Seattle a day before meeting with the Board of Directors about the Clinic. He told her they thought it was arson and that concerned him very much. Kristy agreed and encouraged him to go whenever he needed.

Andy arrived in Seattle a day before his scheduled meeting at the Foundation. Mary was very relieved to see him.

Andy saw the fire damage immediately. It was quite extensive. Andy asked Mary to tell him exactly what happened. She said the dogs started barking loudly about 2 AM and when she looked out the fire was fully engaged.

Mary said she ran out and unlocked all of the cages and all of the dogs got out unharmed. Fortunately, several dogs had been released to good homes the day before.

Mary said she had no idea who would do such a thing. She asked the Fire Captain if he was certain it was arson and he said he had no doubts about it.

Thankfully, the fire department came within about five minutes and put it out. It took them nearly half an hour.

Fortunately, the house wasn't burned.

The farm had full insurance so the damage would be covered. However, since Mary lived there alone, it was very concerning for her. She didn't feel very safe now.

Andy went out and spent some time looking carefully at where the fire started and the damage it did. He was surprised to find what looked kind of like a campsite. There was a burned blanket there, a candle and an empty water bottle. It crossed his mind to wonder if a homeless person had settled there and, perhaps, the fire started by accident. He thought it was a real possibility, in fact.

Mary told him that a homeless man had actually come to her door the day before and asked if there were any odd jobs he could do to get some food. She told him she didn't have any work for him to do but she made him a sandwich.

She didn't think he would be the kind of person who would deliberately start a fire or hurt the animals. He seemed quite appreciative of the food she had given him.

Andy told Mary he would be in town for a few days and suggested that he might stay there at the farm with her. That would likely make her feel safer. She was very happy with that suggestion. She said she would prepare a meal for them around 6 PM.

Andy was happy to stay there at the farm with Mary. He loved spending time with and playing with the dogs. Also, it would give them a chance to talk about veterinarian issues. Andy missed that.

Mary told him she had to let the last veterinarian go because he only seemed to be there to get a paycheck. He just didn't fit in to caring about the dogs or trying to find them good homes. She needed a different kind of person to help her.

Andy suggested maybe he could help her find someone.

That night, all was calm at the farm. Andy was up early, had coffee with Mary and was off to his meeting at the Foundation.

He said he would be finished around noon and would bring some sandwiches back for lunch.

Andy was struck by the sculpture of Corky and Hazel as he entered the Foundation. What sweet memories they were. He missed them both. Andy was so aware of the need to treasure who and what we have when we have it because it won't always be there.

His meeting with the Board of Directors went well. He gave his report and included all of the financial information. At the end, he made a special point of connecting the presence of little Joey at the Foundation and that his mother had sought help at the Clinic regarding domestic violence issues. She had been murdered and Andy had found him walking into traffic on a busy street. He thanked them for including Joey at the Foundation.

Andy made his way to the lunchroom for the purpose of observing Joey. He was sitting with his caretaker, eating his lunch. He was the youngest child at the Foundation. It appeared he was being well cared for.

Andy walked over and placed both of his hands very gently on little Joey's shoulders. He gave him a big smile and said, "Hi, Joey." Little Joey smiled back at him. He seemed to be doing just fine. Andy left feeling reassured that Joey was in good hands and making the necessary adjustments.

After the meeting, he picked up some sandwiches and headed back to the farm. Mary was waiting for him. She seemed subdued and quiet, as though something was wrong.

Andy invited her to share with him whatever was going on for her. She shared with Andy that she was getting older, that she was tired and wondered if it was time for her to give up her dream of sheltering stray dogs.

Andy was very surprised to hear that was how she was feeling. He asked if she thought her feelings had something to do with the fire. She looked away and said, "maybe." She said she was more upset by the fact that it was deliberately set. Somehow that made her feel as though neither she nor the dogs were safe.

Andy asked her how she might feel if he were to hire a night watchman from dusk until dawn. That should give her some peace of mind. She replied, "Do you really think we could find someone who could do that?" Andy was sure they could. In fact, he would start making some calls today. He knew there were a lot of people out of work who would probably jump at such an opportunity.

The first call Andy made was to the Foundation. He asked if anyone there was aware of someone looking for work who might be appropriate for their needs. He was put in touch with Human Resources. They knew Andy well.

"As a matter of fact, I was told just this morning that Rita's son was looking for work. He graduated high school last year." Andy asked for his number. He called him. His name was Jim. He said he would definitely be interested. They made an appointment for him to come to the farm at 3 PM that day.

Andy knew his mother, Rita. She was a good worker. She worked in the food service department at the foundation. She was a very pleasant lady. She had worked there for many years.

Jim was five minutes early for his appointment. He had on clean clothes with hair combed and he was smiling as Mary answered the door. Mary and Andy showed him the kennels and described why they were needing help. The farm was actually pretty close to where he lived. He thought it would be a good job for him. He said he would love spending time with the dogs. He said he had a dog of his own. He offered to feed and water them when he came.

It was Andy's last night to be there. He spent some time with the new night watchman. The two of them did some clean up of the burned kennel area. They managed to create quite a pile of debris and cleaned up the area.

Finally it was dark. Andy thanked him for his help and told him he would be leaving the next morning. He would see him in the morning before he left. They retired for the evening.

Before he knew It, it was time for Andy to leave for the airport. He wrote Mary a check to cover Jim's salary for the next six months. He said he would keep in touch and to let her know if there were any problems at all.

Mary smiled and thanked him for all of his help. She thanked him for being her unseen angel.

When Andy left the farmhouse to go to his car, he made it a point to touch base with Jim and tell him goodbye. He was nowhere to be found.

Andy put his things in the car and began to look for him near the burned kennels. Behind the pile of burned wood they had gathered the night before, he saw Jim, lying on the ground. He could see blood streaked across his scalp and forehead. He was unconscious.

Andy took out his cell phone and dialled 911. Within minutes, he heard the sirens. The paramedics were there and examined him. He was alive but had a nasty wound to his scalp. He was being transported to the hospital.

By that time, Mary was outside, asking Andy what happened. He told her. He let her know that right now he would be following the ambulance to the hospital to find out Jim's condition. This was a very serious assault. He told Mary to go back in the house, lock the door, and wait for him to return.

By the time Andy reached the Emergency section of the hospital, he identified himself and inquired as to Jim's condition. He was asked to take a chair in their waiting room.

It was close to an hour before the doctor came out to talk with him. He said Jim was fortunate that the powerful blow to his head hadn't killed him. He had a serious concussion and would need to remain in the hospital until he improved. Right now they were conducting several tests to assess his condition.

Andy went to the phone and contacted Jim's mother at the Foundation. He told her he would meet her there at the hospital. While he was waiting, he called Kristy and let her know what was happening and that he would be back in a few days. Kristy let him know that everything was going fine, that she loved him and would see him soon.

Andy was beginning to realize that something very major was going on with the farm. Did someone want the property for some reason? Did someone have a vendetta against Mary? Was this about hating animals? What could the motive possibly be?

First a fire, now a violent attack. These people were playing hardball. Would Mary be next?

When Jim's mother arrived at the hospital, she was nearly hysterical. Andy got her some coffee. They sat down and Andy told her all that he knew. He also told her the doctor said they were performing tests and would know more after that. They would have to wait to see him. Andy assured her he would wait with her to find out his condition.

Andy was almost feeling guilty at that time that he had hired a boy to do a man's job. Apparently, whatever was going on at the farm was more serious than he first realized. Apparently, this was a problem that wasn't going to go away anytime soon. He was pondering in his mind what needed to be done to keep Mary and the animals safe.

Just then, Andy's cell phone rang. It was from a long time friend he hadn't talked to in a long time. It was Sara, the realtor. Ironically, she was making an inquiry about the farm. She knew he used to be a co-owner and wasn't certain if he still was or not.

She said the reason she was calling was because she had a client who had made a very generous offer to purchase it.

Andy was stunned. Why all of this sudden interest in a very dated piece of property that housed homeless dogs? Andy asked Sara to tell him more about the buyer. She said that a relative of hers used to own the property and that she just wanted to get it back in their family so their children and grandchildren could enjoy it. It sounded reasonable enough.

Andy asked if he could meet with her and the buyer while she was showing the farm to her. Sara seemed surprised by that question and said she would get right back to him after she contacted the buyer. In less than 30 minutes, Sara called and asked if 1:00 PM that day would work for him. Andy agreed to it and said he would see her then.

Before he left, the doctor came out and gave good news to Jim's mother. His x-rays were clean, there would be no permanent damage. He had a nasty deep cut but the concussion was mild. He would be ready to be discharged that afternoon.

She was told she could see him now.

Andy left and made his way back to the farm. He told Mary what happened and they would be having a potential buyer at 1:00 PM. Mary was very surprised and not certain she was ready to sell. Andy explained that he had cooperated simply because he wanted to get a better feel for why this person was so interested in acquiring the farm now. Maybe it would help them explain the strange events that had been happening. Mary nodded.

Unbeknown to either of them, little Joey's grandfather who was serving a prison term had a cellmate who died in prison.

Before he did, he disclosed that he had grown up on a farm in Seattle. It was where he had stashed all of the money he had stolen before he was caught and sent to prison. It was hidden behind a hidden fireplace.

Joey's grandfather had shared this information with his other daughter, Karen's sister. He told her he would split it with her if they could ever find a way to get ahold of it. He has since been released from prison.

At 1:00 the realtor and the woman made their way to the farm. Andy asked about the family history related to the farm. He was told by the woman that her father's best friend had grown up on the farm and that his last request was to see if it could be owned again by someone who would appreciate how special a place it really was. He said if he had lived long enough, he would have found a way to have bought it himself. Andy simply looked at the woman and believed every word she had just told them was a blatant lie.

Andy and Mary allowed them to walk through and look at the house and the property. Andy told the realtor they would consider her offer and showed them to the door.

Andy immediately called Ralph and said he had a new assignment for him. Ralph was always happy to hear from Andy because he was the most generous client they had.

He asked them to pursue information about Karen's sister and her father and to get back to him ASAP. Ralph confirmed the information with Andy and said he would get right on it.

While waiting to hear back from Ralph, Andy and Mary continued to clean up the yard, feed and water the dogs and spend some time throwing the ball with them.

Andy got a burning permit and lit a match to the huge pile of debris they had collected from the fire. The whole property looked decent again, although there existed far fewer pens for the dogs. They could always be replaced.

At 9:00 PM, Andy's cell phone rang. It was Ralph. He told him that Karen's father had been released from prison a month ago. He was released into his daughter's custody. The two of them were staying in her tiny apartment but neither had been seen in more than a week. Karen's sister was 5'7", 200 pounds, brown eyes, strong build. Her dad was 5'10", 170 pounds, age 59. He had been in prison for grand theft auto issues.

Ralph's description of Karen's sister did not fit at all with the description of the woman the realtor had brought to look at the house. They were nothing alike. This woman was thin, petite, with long black hair and glasses.

Andy couldn't help but notice when the realtor was showing her client the house, she asked specifically about the fireplaces. There were two of them. That seemed to be her only real interest in the house.

That night, after Mary had gone to bed, Andy got out some tools and began tinkering with the two fireplaces. At the end of several hours, he was about to quit when he noticed a small knob clear at the back of one of them that was blackened from soot. It was scarcely visible. With some effort, he reached all of the way back and began to turn the knob. As he did, a side compartment opened out and displayed piles of cash. He was stunned.

Mary was sleeping and he didn't see any need to wake her.

He got a bag and carefully placed all of the money in the bag. There was a lot of money and a pile of gold coins, as well. He made certain he had removed all of it and returned the compartment to its original position.

Tomorrow, he would contact the Foundation's attorney and discuss the legalities of finding the money. He wondered if Mary had a legal right to it since she was the legal owner of the property. He also wondered where the money came from and if there was a statute of limitations on it.

The next morning, while he and Mary were having coffee, Andy told her he had some business to transact at the Foundation but that he would be back in the afternoon and planned to stay with her there at the farm for one more night.

Mary smiled and was very pleased. Andy always made Mary feel safe.

Andy's intelligence and incredible intuitive abilities should never be underestimated. He has an uncanny ability to connect the dots in most every situation.

He paid very careful attention to the buyer's interest in the fireplace, although he knew nothing of the history behind it. It was a very important clue as to why someone wanted the farm and was willing to do whatever it took to get it.

The fire and assault were clever pieces to intimidating an aging, single woman who lived on the property. The timing of the offer to buy the farm was just a little too coincidental, which Andy figured out quickly.

His inclination to check out the fireplaces unlocked the entire mystery. The question now is whether or not the treasure trove found inside can be rightfully claimed by Mary or whether it needs to be turned over to the authorities and traced. Time would tell.

All of Andy's efforts on behalf of Mary and the farm can really be traced back to the day he drove by the dilapidated building where he met Mary and her dogs. Immediately he sprung into action to help her. Those efforts eventually led to obtaining the farm. Now, these actions were to help her either resolve the issues at the farm or find an even better solution. Andy's caring acts can be traced, and deeply appreciated. How fortunate Mary was to have Andy cross her path. Again, maybe this is all really just a part of karma.

Chapter Six

Seeking Answers

Andy was at the Foundation waiting for the attorney to arrive by 8:00 AM. Apologetically, he asked for an hour of his time. Had it been anyone but Andy, they would likely have been refused.

The attorney took copious notes as Andy explained all of the details of the money. In truth, Andy had no evidence that the money had been stolen. The only clue he was ever given had to do with interest in the fireplaces at the farm. He had been tenaciously inspired enough to pursue what he believed was a clue to the fire and attack on Jim at the farm. However, he had no proof.

The potential buyer of the farm had not committed a crime that anyone could prove. If the source of the money could not be traced, there could be no provision for a statute of limitations. At the end of

the hour, the attorney looked at Any and said, "Finders Keepers……"
Andy smiled, thanked him and left.

Andy now had a lot of serious thinking to do. He can just hand all
of it over to Mary since she is the legal owner of the property and it is
her farm.

In fact, it just hit Andy that with that much money, Mary could buy
a much nicer place for the dogs. She could actually go ahead and sell
the farm since they wanted it so badly. She could take that money plus
the new money and find something even more special to carry out her
passionate dream of helping animals.

Andy liked this idea and could hardly wait to tell her.

Andy disclosed to Mary the treasures he found, being careful not to
tell her the exact location. He told her he thought she should contact
the realtor and close the deal. He thought she and Andy could spend
the day looking at new places to house the dogs. Mary was very excited
by that idea.

Mary contacted the realtor, confirmed the generous offer and
accepted it! She wanted the deal to close escrow ASAP.

This was very exciting!

Over the next few hours, Mary and Andy found two new farms
which interested them. They made immediate plans to see them both
that day. They were both in prime areas. They both looked beautiful from
the pictures. They were somewhat close to one another which would
make it easier for them.

Without a realtor, they drove into the first driveway of the first farm.
It was beautiful. It was on 15 acres and had a somewhat dated house
on it. They didn't want to make any decision until they had seen both
of them.

The second property was further out in the country. It had lots
of beautiful trees around it. The 20 acres were fully fenced. It had a
beautifully paved driveway and a lovely very modern looking home with

lots of glass looking out onto the property. It even had a pool. It gave them both a very good first impression.

Inside, it was even lovelier than they had imagined. It was clean as a whistle and everything was modern. All of the appliances were lovely state of the art. It had oak flooring which had just been refinished. It had 4 bedrooms and 3 baths. It was elegant.

Outside there was a section of beautiful pens. They were much larger than the ones Mary had. They were covered and would provide shelter for the animals. It was all first class.

The owners were an elderly couple who had owned the property for more than 30 years. They had raised their family there and had a million beautiful memories, but it was time for them to move on.

They told their realtor that since Mary wasn't using a realtor that they could drop the price by $5,000. Their realtor was comfortable with that offer. They sealed the deal. They did stipulate that the sale was contingent upon the sale of their property but that they did already have a contract for it. That was no problem.

What an incredible day it had been. Mary was beyond ecstatic. Once again, Andy was the unseen angel.

He would sleep peacefully tonight as he hoped Jim would as well. Hopefully, this problem has been solved. His next thought was, "What if I brought little Joey out to meet Mary?....hmmmmmmmm, I wonder how that might go?"

Andy's head hit the pillow and he was out. He awakened feeling rested and he couldn't wait to get back to his family.

Andy and Mary enjoyed coffee together that morning. She was full of gratitude for his wisdom. She could hardly wait for moving day.

Andy could hardly wait to get home.

Once again, it was Andy who knew the importance of obtaining legal counsel regarding the money. If they hadn't been able to keep it, the new farm would not have even been a possibility.

How ingenious of Andy to come up with the idea of putting their newfound funds back into their original investment. As veterinarians, Andy and Mary's compassionate mission to help the dogs was unwavering. That was their mission. That was what had brought them together initially.

Mary has the passion for the animals. Andy has both the passion and the insights to further their mission. They need each other in order to make their dreams come true.

At the new farm, many more animals can be accepted for boarding and finding them new homes. More staff can be hired. More lives can be changed.

Isn't it interesting how, sometimes, things that start our being very naphereous can end up bringing about so much joy, happiness and new beginnings.

It is not always obvious how any of us need to interpret the challenges on our crooked path. Many windings can produce many interpretations. Only as we continue do we come to understand their meaning and purpose. Yet, sometimes, we never do. There are many mysteries.

Chapter Seven

Continuing Challenges

As Andy drove back to the airport, he was aware of the things that were on his plate right now. The Clinic, little Joey and Mary at the farm. That was plenty in light of all the attention his beautiful family needed and deserved from him. He was happy to be going home.

The holidays were just around the corner. This always meant there were many projects going on, especially for the children. Andy and his family always loved the holidays. Kristy made it a point to make it a very special time of year.

Kristy and the children always made very special Christmas cookies. They each made seven and decorated them to their liking. Then they hung them on the tree. The last seven days before Christamas, they got to eat one per day until the day they opened their presents.

They opened each day of their advent calendar which was always kept on the dining room table to help them know exactly when Christmas day would finally be there. This was especially helpful for the younger children.

Kristy and Andy had met and made many friends since they had moved to San Francisco. The whole family loved it there and were happy they had moved. Each of the children had made special friends as had Andy and Kristy. It was a very festive time of year, enjoyed by all.

Unfortunately, Christmas holidays seemed to increase the client load at the Clinic now, including a waiting list. The holidays seemed to be a very stressful time for so many people.

Depression and anxiety loomed large as well as suicidal ideation. It seemed that for some, Christmas was about the saddest day of the year. It seemed to remind people of everything that wasn't in their lives.

Andy seldom heard much from the Clinic. They were very well-trained people who knew how to do their jobs. He was thinking of expanding the number of therapists but there were many bridges to cross before that could be done.

Andy had a certain peace about the Clinic. If it was to expand, the plan would unfold. He was sure of it. He had been shown that truth many times throughout his life.

As many needs as Andy was aware of, he seldom thought about his own. What did Andy need? Right now, he just wanted to take a long nap on the plane and not dream about anything.

It was so seldom there was nothing or no one on his usually very full plate. This was usually when he was asleep. All too soon, Andy was awakened by the pilot's voice to prepare for landing.

He was happy to be home.

Andy felt as though his children had grown while he was away. He didn't like being separated from his family. Separation anxiety had been such a big part of his life. He just wanted to feel safe, loved and at peace.

Kristy made a special dinner that evening. It was the family's favorite. Each of the children had many things they wanted to tell their Dad since he had been away. Dinner was filled with endless chatter. Everyone seemed happy, including Andy.

It seemed the longer Andy lived and got involved in the lives of many others, the more he loved just being at home with his own family. He realized how close he came to losing everything that mattered to him. He was a changed man.

The problem was that he still had the enormously compassionate heart God gave to him which motivated him to reach out to others. It was the reason he rescued children from traffic, helped a woman care for her homeless dogs, took a man and his dog off the streets, and led an organization with a mission to change the lives of traumatized children. Truly, this man is an unseen angel.

After the children were in bed that night, Andy and Kristy sat outside listening to the ocean waves, just holding one another.

They were both quiet. No words needed to be spoken. It was as though they both realized how quickly life was moving. They realized the preciousness of their time together. It would not last forever.

Andy has reached a quiet space on his crooked path. The waters are peaceful and he is assessing where he's been and maybe some semblance of where he wants to go.

Andy would never wish his life on anyone. If he was really honest, he didn't really believe he had a lot of choice about where his path would take him. He wanted to believe that it was all about his choices but he had lived long enough to know that he had encountered challenges on his path he wished had never happened.

Andy would always feel the empty space in his heart from losing his parents. He would always believe that the life and examples they provided him in his first eight years had formed the essence of his character. He felt especially blessed that he got to experience this first hand because of his grandfather.

So much of Andy's life had been spent on intervening in the lives of others. Now, he was in a space of looking inward and investing his energies under his own roof.

Andy's crooked path included losing his parents at an early age, being kidnapped and spending ten years by a ruthless Islamist, having his life threatened for telling the truth, having his son murdered, experiencing a divorce, being in a mental hospital, losing Allison. All of these remembrances were almost too much for him to take in. Andy was tired and just needed to feel his family's loving arms around him. He longed to feel loved, safe and nurtured.

Andy was thinking seriously of resigning his positions from the Foundation and the Clinic. He would continue to be supportive of both of them but it was time for him to hand the baton to the next person.

Andy would soon be turning 60. He was very aware that the sand in his hourglass was continuing and wondered how much was actually left before it would be over.

There was still so much Andy wanted to do. He was at a place on his path where he wanted any challenges to be about his family. That's where he wanted to put his energies.

Summer was coming soon. The children would be out of school. Andy wanted to plan the trip of a lifetime. He and Kristy would spend quality time planning just the right places and time to ensure the best family trip the children would have to cherish for the rest of their lives.

Now, this was something that renewed Andy's spirit and energies. He would share this idea with Kristy and make it a reality!

Chapter Eight

Time Out

Andy and Kristy not only talked non-stop about their impending trip, they decided to involve the children in the planning. They spent hours around their table with maps, charts, graphs, brochures and considered every suggestion from every family member. The children were as excited as they were.

When they finally had managed to pull together what looked like a reasonable itinerary to them, Andy contacted their favorite travel agent. She had done such a phenomenal job of their trip around the world, her help would be invaluable.

Andy placed a call and invited her to the house so that all five family members could participate in the planning. Andy would pay her for her time with them.

Andy had scheduled a four hour block of time with Jane on Sunday afternoon. It was time to put together all of the final details for their trip. It seemed to Andy that all of their ideas might actually mean a trip of about two months. It would really be the trip of a lifetime for all of them. Alice wanted to go to Greece and explore the Greek Islands. Dan wanted to go to Costa Rica and explore the jungle and the animals. He wanted to see a sloth up close and personal. Little Alana wanted to go to Disneyland and meet Donald Duck and Goofy. Kristy wanted to spend some time visiting all of Scandinavia. A lot of her relatives were from that area and she wanted to study her heritage. Andy wanted to go to the Swiss Alps and just take in the serenity and beauty of the area, and do nothing but rest.

When Jane heard all of their ideas, she was quick to say she didn't see any problem at all in putting it all together and making it a reality. She asked for the week to work her magic. They agreed to meet the following Sunday for the same amount of time. The dye had been cast.

The following Sunday, Jane was on time for their meeting. She was carrying five very full packets for each member of the family. It included their full itinerary including travel arrangements, hotels, restaurants and booked activities, including a week-long tour of the Greek Islands.

The trip included everyone's desired destinations. Jane had included Denmark, Sweden and Switzerland, Costa Rica and Disneyland. She even included some time in Hawaii. She had done a masterful job. They could not have been more pleased.

Finally, school was out, Summer was here and they would be leaving in one week. Their first stop was Disneyland. The whole family went shopping together and purchased everything they could think of for their trip. Everyone had a whole new wardrobe.

Very quietly, Andy pondered his own feelings about this trip. He couldn't help but wonder why it was so important to him. He wondered why he had a nagging feeling of some kind of urgency to focus all of his attention and energies on his family. He was experiencing some kind of anxious feelings that just wouldn't let go of him. If he was really honest, he was almost anticipating some kind of catastrophic event not too far down the road. He hoped with all of his heart that he was wrong.

It was the night before they were to leave. All of the packing had been completed and clothes were laid out for each child for the following morning. They were off to Disneyland where they would spend the next four days. Jane had included a dinner where little Alana would have a chance to see a show that included Donald Duck and Goofy. She was already so excited.

It was a very short flight from San Francisco to Los Angeles. All of their airplane trips were booked in First Class. Andy was very grateful his crooked path journey had included lots of financial support so he could make this kind of trip with his family.

The next four days were filled with fun and laughter. Little Alana loved seeing her favorite Disney characters. She had ridden every ride she loved at least two times. By the end of their time there, everyone was ready to move on.

Their next destination was Costa Rica. The whole family was surprised and delighted at the beauty of the area. Colorful birds, beautiful waterfalls, delicious food were loved and appreciated by all. Finally, toward the end of their trip, little Dan still had not seen a sloth. Andy inquired at the hotel where they were staying if they could take some kind of tour that might include the viewing of a sloth. The local zoo was suggested and they were off.

The zoo was like a magical place for each of the children. In fact, they spent three full hours going slowly through it. Kristy had taken multiple pictures of Dan and a sloth. Dan thought that was about the best thing that ever happened to him in his whole life. It made the whole trip for him. Andy even found someone with a polaroid camera to take a picture of Dan and the sloth. He slept with it under his pillow every night.

They had spent a beautiful week in Costa Rica at a 5-star resort.

They felt rested and refreshed and ready to move on. At dinner that last night, Andy requested each family member go around the table and recount what their favorite memory was of the week they had just spent. Everyone seemed to be grateful for very different things.

Kristy's favorite part was being able to just watch her family laugh and enjoy each other. Andy was quick to agree.

As they made their way to their other destinations, there was a strong sense of closeness and love within the family. The children were all getting along well with each other. Kristy and Andy were patient with all of them. The trip couldn't have been going better. It was everything Andy and Kristy hoped it would be.

Their tour of the Greek Islands was a dream come true for Alice. At dinner the first night she commented, "Allison would have loved this cruise.…..I miss her so much." This was somewhat surprising since neither Andy nor Kristy had heard her talk about her twin sister in several years. It helped them understand, once again, the tenderness of her heart and the continued pain of loss in her life.

Sometimes we forget to listen to the people around us. They wondered if she hadn't made comments or her comments had just failed to register with them. Either way, it was a good reminder of what good parenting is all about.

Following their time in the Greek Islands, they were now in Scandinavia. There was so much to see and do. The children especially loved all of the hand-made toys they found. Although they were very expensive, each child was allowed to purchase one toy of their choice. They had to make certain it would fit in their luggage.

Little Alana chose a beautiful handmade doll which actually looked a little like her. Dan had chosen a horse which was hand carved and cost a fortune. Alice chose a chess set which was actually very elegant. Each child was very pleased with their gifts and thanked their parents.

Kristy had brought along with her some detailed information and history of her ancestry who were mostly from this region. She was interested in pursuing one specific relative although she wasn't certain she could find her. It was her mother's half-sister who was nearly 20 years younger than she was. She would likely be more like Kristy's age. Kristy had a name which she had matched to a name in the local phone book.

Kristy had just dialled the number in the phone book to see if she could reach Tina. A woman's voice answered and she identified herself as Tina. Kristy introduced herself as best she could and expressed a desire to meet with her if she had any interest or had time.

Tina surprised her by saying she would be delighted to meet with Kristy. She sounded like a very nice person. She and Tina made plans to meet the following day for lunch. Andy was very happy that Kristy would have the opportunity to actually meet one of her blood relatives. It would be the only one besides her daughter.

Kristy arrived at the outdoor cafe early. Tina had described herself and Kristy hoped she would recognize her. Shortly thereafter, she was very surprised to encounter a young woman who looked very much like herself. They greeted one another warmly.

For the next three hours, Kristy and Tina talked nonstop. They both reviewed their childhood history and brought each other on their lives up to now. It was fascinating for both of them. Tina had always lived in Switzerland. She was a young child when Kristy's mother and father died in the car accident. She knew nothing about Kristy.

At the end of their conversation, they had exchanged addresses, phone numbers, email addresses and a million expressions of gratitude for this unanticipated meeting. It actually meant more to Kristy than she could have imagined. She left feeling a deep sense of gratitude as she made her way back to the family.

Andy and the children were all at the hotel's swimming pool which gave her and Andy a chance to talk. Andy could see and hear what a special time she had meeting Tina. He was very happy for her to have made contact with an actual relative. He said he hoped she could visit them in California.

Their time in Scandinavia passed quickly. They could hardly believe they had actually been there for three weeks. The next day, they headed for Switzerland. They took a train ride through the Swiss Alps. They were all very excited about it. They took dozens of pictures. They could hardly believe all of the majestic waterfalls they saw from the train windows.

They had a delightful lunch on the train. They had all enjoyed the experience of eating different foods from various countries. This was an important educational experience for the children. When they reached their destination, they were all pleasantly surprised with the beauty of Switzerland.

The resort Jane had chosen for them was downright exquisite. It looked like something out of a House Beautiful magazine. They had a suite of rooms. Each child had their own bedroom and bathroom.

These arrangements cost thousands of dollars but Andy didn't care because he knew they could never put a price on his family sharing this beautiful time together. They were creating a treasure trove of unforgettable memories. They would have two full weeks there.

The swimming pool was right outside of their rooms. The children were free to come and go as they liked. The refrigerator was stocked with all of their favorite foods. The children couldn't get enough of the homemade ice cream in flavors they had never heard of before. It was almost a magical time for the whole family.

Andy spent his time just resting. He got caught up on his sleep, enjoyed taking walks with Kristy and just doing some very positive reminiscing that created tons of laughter. This was his dream come true for this trip. This was exactly what he had hoped to create. His heart was full of quiet gratitude.

Finally, they were headed for their last destination. They would be spending a week on Maui in the Hawaiian Islands. As the plane touched down and they made their way to the resort, they were not disappointed in Jane's choice of resorts. It was perfect.

The first night on the island, after the children were asleep, Andy and Kristy got to spend some cherished time together. Andy expressed his feelings that he did not want this trip to end. He knew it had to but there was such a deep longing in him to hang onto his deep feelings of love and connectedness to the people who really mattered to him.

Endings were very hard for Andy. Kristy understood this about Andy and made her best effort to comfort him. Somehow, Kristy sensed that Andy's feelings were running very deep and she wasn't certain if she really could comfort him. He seemed to have some kind of intuitive insight that troubled him. She couldn't help him with that other than to assure her that she would be there to walk with him through whatever it was they needed to face. He squeezed her hand, turned out the lights and they were soon asleep.

The last night of their trip, at dinner, little Dan said, "I wonder how Champion is doing? I miss him. I'll bet he is missing us too. I'm glad we are going home tomorrow." Andy and Kristy looked at each other and smiled. Andy said, "Well, Dan, you'll see him tomorrow. I'll bet he'll just eat you up with wet, sloppy kisses." Sam smiled.

The flight back to San Francisco brought feelings of deep gratitude for this special trip. It had been special for each of them, each for different reasons in different ways.

For Andy, it felt like a miracle trip.

The reason for this incredible family trip was actually found in Andy's insecurities. Due to his own very personal history, he wanted to grab hold of what he could, while he could, to fulfill a childhood dream. His dream was to be part of a loving family. In spite of all of the pain of his journey, he was incredibly blessed to be part of a loving legacy.

It is worth noting that Andy never seems to be able to get go of his insecurities. It is almost part of his DNA. Actually, he has many valid reasons for feeling that way, given his history. His life has actually been some kind of a miracle. He has had a strange mixture of deeply traumatic experiences along with an incredible history of blessings and making a difference for good. What a cooked complex life he has led. What a crooked complex life we all lead!

No matter what lies ahead for Andy and his family, he made a beautiful choice to seize the day, to realize his dreams, form a plan and put a foundation under them. He made it happen! Too often, we give up on our dreams, don't have faith they could ever happen and, so, they don't. Perhaps there is something to the dictum: "Just Do It."

Chapter Nine

Unfolding Challenges

When the family returned home and resettled back into their routine, they resumed their usual life. Champion was thrilled to be reunited with the family. They all agreed it had been a fabulous trip but they were ready to be home.

Andy followed through and resigned his positions, both with the Foundation as well as the Clinic. He stayed on until replacements could be found. They were very sorry to have to let him go but realized he was very serious with his resignations.

Andy devoted his time and attention to his family. He continued to be supportive of all and everything he cared about. He had made arrangements for little Joey and Mary to meet.

Joey was now a regular visitor to the farm and, in fact, he and Mary had bonded into a very close relationship. This pleased Andy very much. Unbeknown to Joey, Mary was seeking some kind of permanent arrangement where Joey could come and live with her. Time would tell.

Alice had graduated high school and was now a senior at Stanford University, Andy's alma mater. They were very proud of her. She was studying biology and wanted to pursue the study of medicine. She was a straight A student. She lived close to home and they didn't see her as much as they liked but enjoyed the time they did have with her.

Dan and Alana were both well-adjusted children. They were growing up very fast, too fast. Andy was deeply aware of their roots now extending more to their friends and the outside world and less to their parents. Andy was feeling old.

In a week, Alice would be graduating college. They had a special family party for her. Andy had bought her a new car which pleased her greatly. It was the convertible she had always wanted.

Although the family was stable and everything seemed to be going well, Andy was simply never able to let go of his sense of impending trauma. Perhaps it was a gift. Perhaps it was a curse. Perhaps it was simply reality.

The day came. The family were on their way to Stanford to attend Alice's graduation. Both Andy and Kristy were thinking of how proud her natural parents would be of her on this day.

It was a short drive down the highway to Stanford. They had driven it dozens of times. It was a simple straight highway with a beautiful drive along the ocean. It was a beautiful day for a drive.

A favorite CD was playing, the sun was shining and the family was on its way to celebrate Alice's graduation. Then, the unthinkable happened.

Before anyone in the car was even aware, they were hit from behind by a semi-truck that had lost its brakes coming down the hill. It hit them so hard, the car flew through the air and landed upside down on the island in the middle of the highway. Everyone was either unconscious or dead.

All of the traffic behind them stopped. Drivers warned the highway patrol the semi-truck was out of control on the highway. There was pandemonium.

A physician in the car behind them rushed to the scene. It was catastrophic. Two of the passengers were deceased. He radioed immediately for two ambulances. They were there in less than five minutes.

Two of the family members were rushed away to Stanford University Hospital. They were both admitted to the ICU. One of them had two broken legs and a severe head injury. The other had severe chest/lung trauma and was on a respirator. They were both very seriously wounded. Neither had regained consciousness.

A week had passed. Kristy was the first to regain consciousness. Alice was in the room at the time. She rushed to Kristy's side with tears running down her face. She grasped her hand tightly and said nothing.

Kristy was blinking her eyes and shaking her head slightly.

She was trying to focus. She did not immediately recognize Alice. It took her several minutes before her vision came into focus and she realized Alice was there. All she could say was, "What happened?"

At that point, Alice lost control. She began sobbing and buried her head into Kristy's chest. She couldn't bring herself to have to be the one to tell her about the accident. She pressed the bedside buzzer, requesting a nurse.

The nurse came in, realized the circumstances and gave Kristy a heavy sedative. Eventually, she closed her eyes and was asleep. This would give Alice time to collect herself and do what had to be done.

It was a few hours before Kristy regained consciousness.

Alice was in the chair beside her. She had been given something to help calm her. She took Kristy's hand and told her there had been a bad accident, that a semi-truck had rear-ended them. She was quick to tell her that Andy was in the ICU on a respirator and had not yet regained consciousness.

Kristy studied Alice's face and asked her next question, "Are Dan and Alana alright?" Alice's head dropped and she simply shook her head from side to side. She didn't want to use the word "dead."

Kristy began screaming. Two nurses entered the room and put a sedative in her IV drip. Alice took some deep breaths and settled back in the chair while the sedative began to work for Kristy.

Alice had been made aware of the crash before the commencement started. She had not even participated. She raced to the hospital and had been there for more than a week. She was absolutely exhausted.

Alice had to identify Alana and Dan at the morgue.Actually, it was hard to do, given the state of their mangled little bodies.

She also had to make final arrangements for them. She was living a nightmare. Her entire world had caved in. She had no idea how she was going to survive her future. This felt as bad as it did to watch her parents be murdered, or hear that her twin sister had died. This felt like hell.

It was another week before Andy regained consciousness. The nurses contacted Alice the minute they knew. She was still camped out in Krisy's room but came immediately.

Alice was actually glad he was on a respirator and couldn't really talk. She entered the room, took a deep breath, took his hand and smiled. Andy had no idea what happened but he was keenly aware that his deep fears had been realized.

Alice made it a point to talk in a very soft and assuring way.

She told him that Kristy was also in the ICU, nearby. She told him she was conscious and making good progress. Andy smiled. He attempted to talk and Alice knew what he wanted to know. She simply touched his face, kissed his forehead and told him to get some rest. She left the room. She simply didn't believe he was ready to hear about the rest of the family.

The next several weeks were some of Alice's darkest days. She attended funerals for both Dan and Alana. She could barely stand up. She was so wrung out and heartbroken. She was trying so hard to be strong for her parents, as they had been for her.

There were no words. Her grief was unspeakable.

Some part of Andy always knew of some kind of impending doom. He knew it. He planned the family trip because of his belief there wouldn't always be a family. He was right.

Now, Andy has lost a second son as well as a biological daughter. "What in the hell does God expect of me? Will it soon be time for me to be able to come down from my cross and expect a few peaceful moments before I die?" Andy was furious.

This is a very huge fork in the road for Andy. Is he going to recover emotionally from this crisis? Has he reached his limits of resilience? Does he have it in him to keep going? Andy realized he had made one previous suicide attempt. Was he ready to try it again? Then he thought about Kristy, his beloved Kristy. He knew in his heart he would have to be there for her. They would have to find some way to get through this walk through hell together. He hoped he was up to it.

Andy just shook his head and wished the crash had taken him too. There were just no words to express his feelings. His heart was filled with rage.

Chapter Ten

Finding A Way

The next several months consisted of finding a way to get through each day for both Kristy and Andy. They had both been hospitalized in the ICU for more than a month. Now they have been transferred to a ward on the floor for rehabilitation. They were in the same room. Both were making progress physically, but not emotionally. Their grief was unfathomable. They were both on antidepressant and benzodiazepine medications. Even with those, they were both barely functioning.

Alice was their absolute rock. She had dropped any ideas of pursuing graduate school for now. She was the eyes, ears, legs and focus for her parents.

They instructed her to sell the house immediately. They could never go back there again. They simply couldn't bear it. The house sold very quickly for nearly twice what they had paid for it. Andy could have cared less about the money. Actually, he could care less for just about anything right about now. His anger continued.

Alice had rented a small house. She continued to take care of Champion although he was not the same dog. He was very depressed. Alice could barely get him to take a walk with her.

Actually, Alice was pretty depressed herself.

Andy and Kristy were both being released from the hospital the following week. Alice was faced with the task of renting a place for them to go and help take care of them. She would hire a full time housekeeper and a full time nurse. She and Champion would move back in with them. This was not going to be easy for any of them.

Alice asked if they wanted her to pull furniture out of storage and they both emphatically said no. Neither of them wanted anything that would remind them of the family that used to be.

Alice was feeling desperate. Her parents were being released and she feared they would fall apart once they were out of their cared-for routine of the hospital staff. She decided to make an intervention.

Alice contacted the therapists at the Clinic and had a consultation with them. Two of them agreed to come to the hospital and spend time daily with Andy and Kristy for their last week of confinement. Alice had no idea if this would work but felt she had nothing to lose.

Alice decided to tell them the morning of the agreed upon visit from the therapists. They were surprised but cooperative. They knew they needed help.

Surprisingly, their visit went well. They discussed the necessity for Andy and Kristy to visit the final resting place of their deceased children. With tears, they agreed.

Alice found a lovely house for them to rent with a nice backyard for Champion. She brought them home on a sunny afternoon. She had rented furniture for the house until they had more permanent plans. They seemed pleased with her choices.

Alice had hired a gardener, a nurse and a housekeeper.

Actually, things seemed to be going pretty well. They had both made remarkable progress physically.

Alice was pleased as she observed Champton nuzzle up to Andy. He reached down and massaged his neck like old times. It brought tears to Alice's eyes.

For the next several months, everyone did their part. The therapy continued. The visit to the cemetery went as well as it could. It seemed they were making progress as best they could. Grief is a formidable opponent.

As time commenced, the therapists were able to get Andy and Kristy to talk about Alana and Dan. They were encouraged to keep a positive focus and cherish their memories. They were encouraged to reminisce and enjoy who they were as little people. They were finally able to do this and it felt good to them.

Kristy and Andy both knew of the deep bond and love they had for each other. Right now, however, both of them were working hard to communicate their love because of their deep emotional wounds. Nonetheless, they never gave up.

One day, Andy got a call on his cell phone from Mary. She had waited several months to place the call. She couldn't have felt worse for their enormous loss of their children. During this call, she didn't mention their loss.

Mary told Andy that Joey was coming to live with her on a permanent basis. All of the pieces had come together which she felt was a miracle.

She had grown so fond of him and was so excited that he would be a permanent member of her life.

Mary told him how well everything was going there at the farm, how the animals were thriving and that they had found dozens of good homes for them. She kept the entire conversation totally positive.

Then, Mary asked if he and Kristy would be open to coming up and helping them celebrate the one year anniversary of the farm and spend some time with little Joey. He remembered Andy and had asked about him. This seemed to please Andy.

He told her he would need to talk it over with Kristy and would let her know. It was a pleasant conversation. Andy was glad she had called. He was especially happy to hear the news about Joey.

Alice was the first to suggest that a trip to the farm in Seattle was an excellent suggestion. What a neat thing it would be for Andy to meet with the child whose life he had saved many years ago. She thought it would do both of them a world of good to go there. She even offered to go with them. Andy looked at Kristy and asked her what she thought. Kristy replied, "Let's do it!"

Alice called Mary the following day and asked when it would be convenient for them to come. She asked if it would be alright if she came too.

Alice was very pleased to get this news. She said they were welcome to come any day at any time of the day or night. She and Joey would meet their plane. They were welcome to stay as long as they liked.

Joey is 10 years old now. It hardly seemed possible. Andy remembered it like it was yesterday. How quickly the years were going by. Andy couldn't have agreed more.

Two weeks later, the plane was touching down. Andy, Kristy and Alice were there to spend some time with Mary and Joey.

It was the first trip anywhere since they had travelled to Stanford for Alice's graduation. It actually felt good to them to be there.

Andy couldn't believe how much Joey had grown. He was a young man now. He seemed so mature. Andy was certain it had a whole lot to do with the care he had received at the Foundation.

Joey seemed immediately drawn to Andy. He took his hand as they made their way to Mary's car in the parking lot. As they reached the car, Joey looked up at Andy and said, "I like you." Andy was surprised. He smiled at Joey and helped him into the car.

When they reached the farm, Andy could not have been more impressed with the condition and all of the changes Mary had made. It was spectacular.

Andy walked the farm with Mary. The pens were immaculate. The dogs looked clean and healthy. There were several workers, cleaning the pens and playing with the dogs. He could not have been more impressed. He asked her how she did all of that by herself.

Mary explained that after she purchased the farm, several benefactors had generously donated to the mission of the farm. This enabled her to hire two part-time veterinarians and several staff members. They all seemed to have a real caring of the animals and worked together very well. They had grown to capacity.

Mary commented that she had heard the new owners of the old farm had put it up for sale again shortly after they took possession. She guessed they were disappointed. She laughed when she said it. Andy understood exactly what she meant.

Andy told Mary in confidence that he and Kristy had received over 100 million dollars in compensation for the horrible accident that took their children's lives. He said he would like to donate ten million of it to her farm. Mary turned as white as a sheet. Then she gave Andy a huge hug. That would enable her to carry out her dream for the next phase of the farm.

Mary wanted to create a program for traumatized children to be able to come and interact with the animals. It would be a healing kind of endeavor. In fact, she wanted to present it to the Foundation and include all of their children. Andy smiled.

Andy also wanted to make contributions to both the Foundation and the Clinic. He wanted it to go toward the cause of helping hurting children. Andy was actually beginning to feel some of his caring spirit returning. Kristy sensed this and was grateful they had made the trip.

Alice had been spending time observing the veterinarians treat the animals. It crossed her mind to consider the field of treating animals rather than people. Andy was happy to observe this change in Alice. He was beginning to see real purpose in their visit to the farm and was glad they had made the trip.

Andy and Kristy are hanging on by a thread. Alice is providing strength they need in order to keep going. She had intervened to get some help from therapists at the Clinic which have proved to be invaluable.

Burdens have fallen on Alice that she could never have foreseen. Why, indeed, had she and her sister been adopted into this family? She could see the purposes, although she would never have consciously chosen them. This is not so unlike how life is for most of us. We don't see the purpose up close and personal but sometimes we can see it in retrospect.

Mary and Andy are unlikely friends. Had it not been for Andy's compassion with animals, he would never have reached out to Mary and her dream of helping homeless dogs. Now, all of these years later, she is the caretaker of a child he once rescued from death and is a motivator for his healing from an incident worse than death. It is all part of the complex crooked path.

Chapter Eleven

Starting Over

Andy, Kristy and Alice had stayed at the farm for a month.

None of them could believe they had stayed that long. The time had passed so quickly. Little Joey was thrilled with their visit. He did not want them to leave.

Before they did leave Andy assured Joey that they would come back soon. He bought Joey a cell phone and programmed his number into it. He taught him how to push the right buttons and be connected to Andy. He told him he was welcome to call him at any time. Joey smiled.

When it came time to leave, Kristy, Andy and Alice were all in agreement that they were leaving in much better shape than they were when they came. It had really been a therapeutic visit. It helped Andy and Kristy realize their need to keep reaching out.

On the plane ride back, Andy and Kristy had a serious conversation about their future. Where did they want to live now? Were they ready to look for permanent housing? What were their future aspirations?

Kristy expressed some interest in wanting to get back into the classroom and continue teaching. She loved children and she loved teaching. It helped her feel as though she was making some kind of positive difference.

Andy asked her where she saw them living. Surprisingly, Kristy expressed some interest in moving back to Seattle.

Somehow, their life in San Francisco had been such an incredible gift. However, that dream had come to an end and it was time to move on.

Their best friends lived in Seattle. The Foundation was in Seattle. Kristy and Andy had met in Seattle. Mary and Joey were in Seattle. There were a lot of things going for a move back there.

Andy's parents and grandparents' houses had been sold.

He had lived a few lifetimes in San Francisco. He knew, however, that it would never be the same again without little Dan and Alana. He was open to moving back. Also, they would be near Joey and the farm. We would have an opportunity to be part of his life. This appealed to Andy. It was settled.

As soon as they returned to San Francisco, they gave notice to vacate their house in two months. This gave them time to choose a new home in Seattle and continue their journey on their complex crooked path.

Alice was completely on board with the move back to Seattle. It was where she had grown up. In fact, she was kind of excited about the move. Shortly, they would make the trip to find housing. For now, she was content to continue living with her parents and ensuring her help with whatever they needed. It was very important to her to be a good daughter. In fact, maybe she could even pursue her schooling and become a veterinarian, like Andy.

Their trip to Seattle was preceded by an exhaustive internet search of available housing. The three of them had selected three homes they wanted to see.

They wanted to see all three of them before making any decision. Andy had made the arrangements for each of the viewings. They were all happening on the same day, spaced two hours apart for each. All of them had backyards surrounded by water.

All three of the homes were beautiful. However, one of them won their hearts. It was the one they chose. They made a cash offer, would close escrow in less than 30 days and the house would be theirs.

Their best friends, Tony and his wife were ecstatic they were moving back to Seattle. In fact, the home they had chosen was close to theirs. Already, this was feeling good to everyone.

The month passed quickly. Their plane was just about to touch down at the Seattle airport. They would get all new furnishings for their new home. This really was a new beginning for them. Although both Andy and Kristy continued to carry the pain of the loss of their precious children, they both really believed that one day they would be reunited with them. They took great comfort in that belief.

Alice and Kristy thoroughly enjoyed their shopping trips for the new house. They were very pleased with the new furnishings they had chosen. Most of it had been delivered and looked amazing. In fact, everything looked perfect.

That night at dinner, after they said the blessing, Kristy commented that she could really hardly believe where they were and the progress they had all made. They all agreed it was nothing short of a miracle.

Alice renewed her teaching credential in Washington and had sent resumes to several schools in the area. Before she knew it, she had two interviews. She was very excited. She was ready to start giving again.

At some level, she hoped it would help her heal the empty spaces in her heart.

Before they knew it, Kristy had a new job, Alice was enrolled in vet school and Andy was building a relationship with Joey. Life was moving on, although not without great effort on all of their parts.

Andy, Kristy and Alice had all miraculously regrouped. It was almost an unbelievable scenario. Their recoveries represented the exception, not the rule. They were amazing people.

For most of us, we usually find out what stuff we are made of when we observe our responses to the stresses of our crooked windings. Sometimes we don't like what we see. Nevertheless, we are forced to deal with them, no matter what!

Andy, Kristy and Alice have all pulled together to gather the broken pieces of their collective souls. There is an amazing story.

It is amazing that Andy has the resilience and the desire to form a relationship with little Joey. This is very significant. He seems to have an undaunting and boundless caring spirit. If only we had more Andys in the world.

It took courage for Andy, Kristy and Alice to let go of their life in San Francisco and move to Seattle. They are making a real effort to move on with their lives. They seem to find a way to make a difference for good wherever they go. That is a rare gift. Andy has already been an amazing gift to little Joey. He once saved his life. Now, they are developing a relationship. Perhaps he will come to be a comfort to Andy since losing his son, Sam.

The complex crooked path has many windings....and who can know it?

Chapter Twelve

Life at the Farm

Andy found himself at the farm on many days. He usually showed up after Joey came home from school. He made it a point to ask him about his day and always helped him with his homework. Joey had come to count on Andy being there for him. They were forming a close relationship.

Unbeknown to anyone, Joey's biological grandfather and aunt had bought and moved into Mary's old farm. Although they never found any money in the fireplace, they had tracked down Joey's whereabouts. They knew he was being raised at a place called the Foundation. They knew it was a very expensive facility and they were trying to find out how he came to be placed there.

They had learned about Andy rescuing him and eventually being the one responsible for his care at the Foundation. His aunt had actually gone to the Foundation to find out more information about him. They were turned away by the Foundation's legal department. They were not allowed to reveal personal information about any of their residents.

Joey's aunt was never close to Joey's mother. She nor her father had any real interest in Joey's welfare. They saw him as a potential source of income. Apparently, someone with money had taken an interest in him. They wanted to find that person.

Shortly after that, there was a break in at the Foundation.

The attorney's office had been searched. Joey's file was missing. They immediately knew who the suspect was. However, they couldn't prove it.

The attorney contacted Mary to let her know what had happened. She was grateful to have the information.Mary was in the process of legally adopting Joey. Their final court date wasn't for another month.

Mary contacted Andy immediately when she hung up from the attorney at the Foundation. These people had gone to great lengths to learn the whereabouts of Joey. They were dangerous people. Joey's grandfather was a convicted felon.

Andy believed Joey to be in danger at this point. He felt very protective of him and wanted to do whatever he could to keep him safe. Even if they found him, they had no legal rights to him although his safety had not been yet legally secured.

That day, Andy went to the farm anticipating Joey's arrival from school. He wasn't on the bus. Mary called the school immediately. They were told he was at school, had attended all of his classes and was dismissed to go to the bus after school.

Apparently, he never made it there. The bus driver said he had not seen him.

Mary contacted the police. Andy witnessed her conversation. They agreed to come to the farm and take a report but they really wouldn't be able to do any kind of formal investigation until he had been missing for more than one day.

Andy understood but was very upset by this fact.

Andy told Mary to wait at the farm for the officer and give them a missing person's report. Andy said he was going to drive to the old farm and see what he could learn.

Andy's mind was racing. Hadn't Joey been through enough already? Andy was angry. Actually, he didn't trust himself right now. He was so angry.

Andy knew he had to regroup before he reached the farm.

There was no point in him being an irrational confrontive madman. That wouldn't help anyone.

When Andy reached Mary's old farm, he noticed an old red pickup parked in the dirt. He didn't notice any activity on the property. It looked very rundown. He parked far away and walked to the back of the farm. He didn't want to be noticed.

The lights were off. It didn't look as though anyone was home. About an hour later, he noticed a car pull into the driveway. The driver was a young woman and there was a man in the passenger seat. In the backseat was Joey!

They all got out of the car. Andy made his presence known at that time. Joey saw him and called out to him, "Hi, Andy. See what I just got!" He was holding up a new gameboy in his hand and had a huge smile on his face.

Andy approached him. He said he had just met his aunt and his grandfather. They took him to McDonalds and let him order anything he wanted. Then they went shopping and bought him a new gameboy. He was a very happy little boy.

Andy put Joey behind him and introduced himself to the aunt and grandmother. He made it very clear that people were worried sick about Joey. He told them they had no right to take him. He took Joey by the hand and told him they were leaving.

The aunt and grandfather just looked at each other. Finally, his aunt said, "We're sorry.....we didn't mean to worry anyone...We were just very excited to see him again...."

Andy didn't even bother to respond to her. He turned and pulled Joey as they walked swiftly down the driveway to his car. On the way back to Mary's farm, Joey asked Andy why he was so mad. Joey just told him how nice they were to him, took him to get food and bought him a nice toy. He didn't understand why that was a problem for anyone.

As Andy listened to Joey and pondered his remarks on their way back to the farm, he realized that he and Joey and Mary needed to have a serious talk. Although Andy was only ten years old, he would have to hear some difficult facts about his family.

Andy had telephoned Mary and let her know he was returning to the farm with Joey. They would be there in a few minutes. He said he would explain when he saw her.

Mary was frantic when they drove into the driveway. She ran to the car and hugged Joey. Joey didn't understand any of what was going on. He thought everyone was acting very strangely.

Andy picked Joey up and placed him on his lap. He explained to Joey that it was time for him to hear and understand some facts about his life. He asked Joey if that would be okay.

Joey looked at him, wide-eyed and hesitant. He looked at Mary who had a distressed look on her face.

Andy explained to Joey that the first time he met him was about seven years ago when Joey had wandered into traffic on a busy highway and was in real danger of being hit by a car.

He asked him if he remembered. He didn't.

Andy explained that he was by himself. There was no one with him, taking care of him. Joey asked, "Where was my Mommy?" Andy took a deep breath and said, "I don't really know where she was." Andy looked at Mary when he said it.

After that, you went to the Foundation where they took care of you. "Do you remember the Foundation Joey?" he asked. "Yes, of course I do." "Do you know why you were placed at the Foundation?" Joey answered, because "My Mommy couldn't take care of me anymore." Andy replied, "Yes, that's right." Do you know why she couldn't take care of you?" Joey's eyes filled with tears and he said "Cuz she's dead." He began to cry.

At that point, Andy and Mary knew they needed to take a break. Mary suggested some ice cream. She said she had just bought a new container of his favorite ice cream that very day. She even bought some sugar cones to put it in. Joey smiled and asked for one, "Please" he said.

Joey still sat on Andy's lap while he ate his ice cream. They all had ice cream together and tried to lighten the mood.

Eventually they needed to return to their conversation.

"Joey, do you know why your Mommy died?" Joey said, "No." He just understood that she did and that he had to go to the Foundation to be cared for.

Andy didn't see any point in upsetting Joey with the facts about his Mother's death. He did, however, know that he had to make Joey understand that the people who took him today were not good people, no matter how well they treated him.

Andy asked Joey, "Do you know who the people were today who took you to McDonalds and bought you the gameboy?" Joey said, "Yes, they were my friends." Mary asked him, "How do you know they were your friends?" Joey replied, "Because they told me they were and they were nice to me."

Andy asked Joey to look at him. He said, "The people who took you today were your grandfather and your aunt. They were related to your mother. They, unlike your Mommy, are not good people. They tricked you. They really don't care about you.

Mary and I are the ones who are your real friends. We love you Joey. You must never go with those people ever again. They can hurt you." He asked Joey if he understood.

Joey asked, "Well, why were they nice to me?" Andy told him it was because they wanted him to like them so they could hurt you. It had been awhile since Andy had any discussions with a ten year old. He was struggling with how to phrase his sentences. "You must never go with them again. If you ever see them again, you need to tell Mary or me, okay?"

Joey looked at Mary, then at Andy and said "okay." He jumped off of Andy's lap and went outside to play with the dogs.

Andy was exhausted. He realized he wasn't used to dealing with children and their issues anymore. He was out of practice.

Mary reassured him he was doing fine.

It costs to care.

Andy's efforts with looking after Joey were exhausting for him. At the same time, caring is what kept Andy going. It was simply who he was.

Part of Andy's drive in looking out for Joey was, in part, a projection of his own childhood. He had longed for someone to care for him at a time when no one did. It would always be in his nature to be protective of the little people.

Besides, Joey has become a real person to Andy. He isn't just a little boy Andy is trying to help. He has become someone whom Andy genuinely cares about and wants to nurture and protect. In fact, Joey may be, in part, a comfort to Andy because of the loss of his two younger children. This would be a pain that would follow him forever.

Andy couldn't have been more delighted that Joey and Mary were becoming a team. He would be Mary's legal beneficiary of the farm one day. It was a very important piece of property. He had much to learn over the next ten years of his life. His journey had just begun.

Andy was committed to helping Joey and Mary in any way he could while he still could.

Chapter Thirteen

The Good Life....

Life in Seattle was proving to have been a very good decision for Andy and his family.

Alice was having a great experience studying veterinary medicine. She had decided to specialize in equine medicine.

She loved horses. In fact, that would be her next birthday present from her parents. They knew how excited she would be.

Kristy was finding great satisfaction in being back in the classroom. She loved teaching. It gave her a strong sense of strength in believing she was really making a significant contribution to helping children find their way. She was a very natural nurturer and the children loved her.

Andy had gotten more involved at the farm. It gave him a chance to practice his veterinary skills and spend time with the dogs. He genuinely enjoyed being around and playing with them. He loved delivering puppies. He especially enjoyed watching Joey loving them so much. In fact, Joey was expressing interest in one day being able to care for the dogs himself. He paid careful attention to Andy's work with the dogs. He was a very bright little boy. He had a bright spirit and a compassionate heart.

Joey had not had any more interactions with his aunt or grandfather. Andy was hoping he had made a strong enough impression that they would never try to interfere in his life again.

Life seemed to have taken on a quiet quality again, something he thought would never be possible. Andy was grateful although he would never have the same level of peace or his feelings about life itself ever again. Losing his children had a very strong and lasting impact on him.

One morning as he was on his way to the farm, his cell phone rang. It was from Kristy's school. They said that she had collapsed in the classroom and was taken by ambulance to the hospital. This news broke Andy's heart.

He drove as fast as he could to the hospital and parked illegally in the Emergency parking area. He raced through the doors, identified himself and asked for information about his wife.

He was asked to wait. The doctor was with her now. When he was finished, he would come and talk with him. Andy took a deep breath as he took his seat. It felt to him like he had been down this road way too many times. He felt weary.

It seemed as though it took forever before he heard his name being called to speak with the doctor. He was not prepared for what he was about to hear.

Andy was told they had taken some x-rays and it appeared that Kristy's cancer had returned. They found a large mass in the wall of her chest. His concern was whether or not it had metastasized since she had collapsed. They were doing additional tests and would know more by tomorrow. The doctor had also ordered a CT scan. For now, he had decided to admit her to the hospital in order to stabilize her and determine the extent of her illness.

Andy asked if he could see her. The doctor said he could but advised him to make his visit short. She really required rest right now. She had been given a sedative.

Andy entered the room and approached her. Her eyes were closed and she was very pale. He leaned over and kissed her on the forehead and put his hand on hers. She opened her eyes, but said nothing. There were no words for either of them.

Andy watched as he saw the tears running down the sides of her face. His own eyes teared up. He leaned down, told her he loved her and that she should sleep now. He left.

As Andy was driving home he realized he was dreading having to tell Alice about Kristy's condition. Alice heard the garage door go up and came out to greet Andy. She was in an exceptionally good mood and told him that she had made the honor roll. He hugged her and congratulated her.

Immediately, Alice asked, "What's wrong?" Andy just looked at her and shook his head. He burst into sobs. They went into the house and sat at the kitchen table. When he was able to speak he told her what happened. Alice struggled to hold back her tears. She didn't say anything. She got up from her chair, went to the back of Andy's chair, put her arms around him and laid her head on his shoulder. She stayed there for several minutes. This was just way too much stress for either of them to have to handle. They were losing their family, one person at a time.

The next day when Andy went to the hospital and found his way into Kristy's room, he found her crying. The doctor had just left. He told her about her test results.

The cancer had metastasized and he estimated she probably had less than six months to live. Andy closed his eyes, stopped dead in his tracks and said nothing.

Kristy said they were offering radiation therapy and chemotherapy and would need to know soon if she was inclined to follow that course of treatment.

Andy wanted her to do absolutely everything she could to stay alive. Kristy just looked at him and slowly shook her head from side to side. "No, Andy....I just can't."

Kristy lasted only three months. Alice and Andy did everything they possibly could do for her. She had around the clock care at home. They hardly left her side.

Kristy died peacefully in her sleep. The only comfort Andy could muster was to believe that she was in the presence of their precious children now. Alana and Dan had their mother back.

Kristy had asked to be cremated and wanted her ashes scattered at her children's graves. Andy would make certain that her wish was carried out, but not yet. He just couldn't handle it right now.

Andy had never had the feelings he was struggling with now. Somehow, this was different. He felt as though his whole reason for living was gone. He never felt more alone in his life.

For days, Andy just sat in his favorite chair in the family room, staring out at the water with vacant eyes. His soul was shattered.

Who would have ever believed that Andy's beloved family would be reduced to just him and his adopted daughter?

Andy was out of energy and out of cope. He sat in his chair for a solid week. He spent hours looking out at the water.

Andy has endured more trauma, loss and death than would be fair for any human being. However, life is not fair and there are, in fact, people who endure greater pain and tragedy than others.

In fact, the more relationships we form and the more we bond with others, the more vulnerable we are to trauma and loss.

We grieve to the extent that we have loved. It is a special challenge to lose people we love. The famous five stages of grief are not easily accomplished. Somehow, the challenge is to find a way to accept the loss and not let it destroy us.

It is very empowering to be able to reframe our loss in such a way that we can stay focused on all of the love and empowerment that our loved one gave to us. Moving forward is part of our way of honoring that love and those losses.

Finding a way to channel our grief in a positive way is a great strength in helping us find a way to move forward. This is the challenge Andy faces now.

Chapter Fourteen

Finding a Way

Joey was so happy to see Andy. He raced to his car, took him by the hand and said he wanted to show him something. He led him out to the dog pens and showed him a new litter of puppies. They were Old English Sheepdog puppies. They were beautiful. Joey picked up one of the puppies and said, "This is Brutus. He's my favorite." This made Andy smile, his first smile in weeks.

Andy picked up one of the puppies. It felt good to him to hold a sweet little puppy so new to the world. It warmed his heart to see Joey so transfixed by the puppy. Andy suggested that maybe it was time for Joey to have his very own dog. They would have to run the idea by Mary first. Joey was so excited by this idea, he took the puppy and ran into the house to find Mary.

Shirley J. Gilbert, PH.D.

Mary said it was time for lunch. She, Alice, Andy and Joey were seated at the table outside. The conversation was kept at a surface level mostly. Mary asked Alice if she was enjoying her veterinarian studies.

Mary mentioned to Andy that she was short a veterinarian and sure could use his help over the next few weeks. One of their veterinarians had found a full time job and his last day was last Friday. She asked Andy directly if he would be willing to give the farm some help for the next few weeks or so. Joey chimed in and said, "Yes, Andy, Yes. We need you." Andy smiled. He said he would be happy to come out and help them for a few weeks.

Alice asked Mary if she had ever thought of adding a section at the farm devoted to horses. She told her she was very interested in equine medicine and would love to work at the farm. Mary indicated that they did, in fact, have room for an equine program. She said she would need to think about it.

In fact, they had six horse stalls already from when the previous owners were there. Andy suggested maybe they could all discuss it later after things were in order for the dogs. Mary thought that was a good idea.

After Alice left the table, Andy told Mary that Alice would be getting a horse for her birthday and that it would be great if they could board him there at the farm. Mary smiled and thought that might actually be a good way of starting the equine program there at the farm. This pleased Andy.

It would be a wonderful way to use up some of the wasted space that wasn't being used now. They had plenty of room to start such a program. In fact, it might be a program the Foundation would be interested in.

The children from the Foundation would probably love to come to the farm and learn about horses. It could become a very educational and practical part of the farm. It would be an exciting way to expand their program, especially if Alice wanted to start such a program. It was an exciting idea, one they were all interested in pursuing.

For the next few weeks, Andy came to the farm every day.

Joey was especially happy to see him and stayed by his side. He loved to watch Andy and learn from him. Andy made it a point to explain to Joey some of the specific things he did to help the animals. Joey had even gotten a special notebook to record things he wanted to remember.

This week-end was Alice's birthday. Andy thought he would like to have her gift waiting for her there at the farm. He asked Mary if it would be OK to house the horse there at the farm. She smiled and said that would be fine. Joey was excited to have a new animal at the farm.

The horse was a two year old Arabian. He thought it would be just perfect for Alice. He was eager for her to see him. Andy made arrangements to have him delivered there the following day. This was a distraction which Andy really needed to get his mind off of his grief over losing Kristy.

Andy arrived at the farm very early that day. He had asked Alice to come to the farm around noon. He said he and Mary had been discussing an equine program and wanted to discuss it with her. He didn't even acknowledge her birthday before he left. He wanted it to be a complete surprise.

At noon, Alice arrived at the farm. Joey ran to her car to greet her and said, "Come see….we have a surprise for you."

Andy and Mary also came out to greet her. Alice looked at her Dad and said, "What's this I hear about a surprise?" Andy smiled, took her by the hand and said, "Follow me." He told her to close her eyes. He led her to the stall where her new horse was housed. Once in front of him, he told her to open her eyes. She screamed with excitement, "Oh, Dad, it's the best present I've ever had. I love him."

Andy had a saddle on him. He opened the door of his stall and led him out in the open. Alice could hardly believe how beautiful he was. Immediately, she mounted the horse and they were off for a ride. They were gone for nearly 30 minutes. They returned and all Alice could say was, "Wow, Wow, Wow."

In truth, this was just what Alice needed to lift her spirits. She worked hard around Andy not to let him see how sad she was over the death of Kristy. Getting her a horse was just about the best therapy she could possibly imagine. She went over and gave Andy the biggest hug.

Alice had prepared a beautiful birthday lunch. She had ordered a very special birthday cake from Seattle's finest bakery. The entire lunch was delicious and it was the most positive conversation between her and Andy they had since losing Kristy. They missed her and wished she could have been there, but they also believed maybe she was there.

About that time, little Joey looked at Alice and asked her, "Will you be my sister?" Everyone at the table laughed. Alice replied, "Of course I will, little brother." Everyone's heart was smiling for just a moment.

What a beautiful day it had been. Alice had to get back to class. Andy was done working for the day. He made it a special point to thank Mary for making the day so special. He was very appreciative. Joey seemed the happiest of all. It was clear that these were the people he considered to be "his family." He loved each of them. They were what made his little world work.

Andy was very grateful for the farm. It gave him a place he loved to go, and people he really cared about and enjoyed being around. Mary had told Andy before he left that day that the following Saturday was Joey's birthday. She invited Andy and Alice to dinner. She said she was planning to give Joey permission to have Brutus as his very own puppy. It would be good training for him to assume the responsibility for caring for a dog.

Very slowly, the life blood of the family seemed to be returning to Andy's home. He was beginning to understand the concept of taking in all of the love and joy that Kristy brought to his life and allowing it to shine through the way he lived his life.

Andy and Alice were both making an adjustment reaction to the recent trauma of yet another death in their family. They had suffered a lot of loss, much of it through trauma. Life's lessons are sometimes so very harsh.

Life at the farm works for Andy in a few different ways. It enables him to practice a seldom used set of veterinary skills. It gives him a social and familial framework to continue relating with others in almost a family setting. His attachments to Joey and Mary are growing.

Before her death, Andy and Kristy had discussed how she hoped life would be after she was no longer with them in the same way as when she was alive. She wanted them to feel her presence and her love everyday. She wanted them to feel her support in whatever way they needed to be supported. She wanted them to feel the love they shared as a family when they visited the cemetery.

Andy has had to make more adjustments than most people.

He had to find ways to survive trauma more than most people. He had to find ways to keep going more than most people.

Andy is an amazing man, an amazing unseen angel.

Chapter Fifteen

Moving Forward

Over the next months and years, Alice graduated from veterinary school, Joey celebrated his 18th birthday and Andy had become a full time veterinarian at the farm.

The equine program was up and running. Andy had managed to establish a program for the children at the Foundation to be part of a weekly training program which they loved.

The farm now had six beautiful horses. Andy and Alice had spent many months training them to be gentle and appropriate for the children. They had hired trained guides when the children were present. It was about the best idea any of them had ever come up with. It was a very healing time for the children. They bonded with both the horses and the dogs. It provided hope and healing for many of the children. Once again, it was part of making a difference for good, something which pleased Andy and Mary immensely.

That morning, before she left the house to run errands, Alice told Andy there was something she wanted to discuss with him at dinner that night. She said she was cooking something special and would see him around 6:00 PM. Andy agreed and said he would see her again. He really had no idea what was on her mind.

At dinner that night, Alice had prepared his favorite meal. When they had finished, Andy asked her what she wanted to discuss. At that point, she reached out in front of him with her left hand. On her ring finger was a beautiful diamond ring. She told him she was engaged to be married during the coming holidays.

Andy was quite taken back. He knew she had been dating but had no idea there was anything serious going on. He could not have been happier for her. He suggested they have him over for dinner soon so that Andy could get to know him. Alice smiled and said they would do that very soon. She told Andy that his name was Mike and that he was from the Bay area of California.

Andy left for the farm feeling somewhat puzzled by Alice's news. It wasn't like her to hold back information from. him. Or, maybe she had tried to tell him and he just wasn't listening.

Either way, he was anxious to meet the young man.

The following week-end, Mike was coming to dinner. He drove a maroon-colored sports car. Alice said it was his pride and joy. They had actually met on a blind date about six months ago. One of her friends was dating a guy who had a friend coming to town and was looking for a date for a band they wanted to hear.

Reluctantly, Alice had agreed to go. Initially, she wasn't very impressed with him but, since that time, he had found a way into her heart. Andy just listened while she explained her relationship with him.

He wondered how well they really knew each other in such a short time. He would withhold judgment until he met him.

Mike came for dinner the following night. He was a good looking man who seemed to know all of the right things to say and do. He was smooth, a little too smooth for Andy's taste. His immediate gut response to Mike was negative. He didn't trust him. Andy wished so much that Kristy had been there to meet him. She was rarely wrong when it came to assessing people's character.

After dinner, Alice and Mike left together to meet some friends at a Club. Alice kissed Andy on the cheek and said she would see him later. She told him not to wait up for her.

After they left, Andy found himself feeling somewhat disturbed after meeting Alice's fiance. Somehow, he had a very uneasy feeling about him and he wasn't at all sure why he felt that way. There was just something about him that didn't quite ring true. He would try to keep an open mind about him and not say anything about it to Alice for now.

About a week later, Andy was driving past Mary's old farm.

He couldn't help but notice a maroon-colored sports car, the same make as Mike's. Andy stopped his car from a distance and sat there, just staring, for nearly an hour. Then he saw Mike come out of the house and get into the car. This troubled him greatly.

That night at dinner with Alice, Andy encouraged her to tell him more about him. Specifically, he was interested in who he knew in town and what had brought him to Seattle.

Alice looked at him and said, "You know, I don't really know the answer to that question. I guess I never thought to ask him that question. I don't know what brought him to Seattle. I just know he used to live in the Bay area." Andy smiled and was quiet.

Although he hated to do it, Andy's next call was to Greg. He just felt he had to know more about Mike before he was going to let his daughter marry him. Specifically, he was interested in knowing the connection between him and Joey's aunt and grandfather. That just seemed like way too big a coincidence to Andy. Greg said he would look into it and get back with him by the end of the week.

The week went by slowly for Andy. He was troubled by this whole scenario. Either way, he could see Alice getting hurt and that was the last thing he would ever want for her.

Around 8:00 PM, Friday night, Andy's cell phone rang. It was Greg. Fortunately, Alice wasn't home and he was able to speak freely.

Greg started the conversation with, "Well, Andy, it's not good. The grandfather and granddaughter both have police records. He served eight years for grand theft auto. She served two years for solicitation and prostitution. They are several months in arrears for the farm they purchased. They will soon be evicted if they can't come up with some money.

As for Mike. He is a wheeler-dealer, a high roller. He also served time for passing bad checks and for money laundering. It seems he worked for a guy who worked out of a Gentlemen's Club who was eventually convicted of breaking and entering and shot through the head, but survived. Andy nearly dropped the phone.

Someone had managed to put all of these pieces together, traced it back to Andy and his family. Now they had found a new way to approach his family. They were after Alice.

This was terrible news. On the other hand, Andy was so glad he had trusted his instincts and had Mike investigated. Now he better understood why he saw his car at the old farm. All of the pieces were coming together. They tried getting at him by taking Joey. Now they were after Alice. How was he ever going to break this news to her? He didn't know. He just knew it had to be done. Actually, he was thinking of inviting Jeff to the house and asking him to tell her directly what he had learned about Mike. The dye was cast.

Andy invited Greg to the house on Sunday afternoon. He told Alice he needed some time with her and scheduled it with her.

Alice had no idea what was going on. She had never met Jeff before. Andy introduced them and told her he was a private detective. He went on to tell her that he thought she needed to hear some things he had discovered. They concerned Mike.

Alice had a troubled look on her face.

Andy tried to prepare Alice for what she was about to hear. He prefaced by telling her about the day he first noticed Mike's car at Mary's old farm and then saw him come out of that house and get into his car. Alice was listening intently. Andy asked if she remembered who had purchased that property. She nodded.

He reviewed the problem with them taking Joey from school without permission. Again, she nodded.

At that point, Andy turned the conversation over to Greg. He explained the history of Joey's aunt and grandfather. He went on to explain the history of Joey's paternal father. Eventually, he explained Mike's history to Alice. He was even able to show certified paperwork backing up his claims.

Andy watched Alice's eyes fill with tears. Then she put her hands over her face. She said, "No, no, no, no, no……."

She got up, left the table and left the room. Andy and Greg sat in silence for several minutes.

A few minutes later, Alice returned to the room and told them she had called Mike and that he was on his way over.

Andy knew that they were headed toward a major confrontation. He was very glad Greg was present as a witness. Andy knew he would need to work overtime in order to stay rational and calm.

He also knew he would be able to do that.

Mike arrived. Alice met him at the door and opened it for him. Andy introduced him to Greg and they all sat down at the table. Alice said, "Tell him what you told me."

Andy began by telling Mike he had observed him getting into his car on the property of Mary's old farm where Joey's aunt and grandfather live. Since they had once taken Joey without permission, he had personally warned them to stay away from him and his family. How do you know them?"

Mike said, "I used to work for a man who was married to her sister." Andy asked, "Who was that man?" Mike said "Just some man that used to work out of a Gentleman's Club in the Bay area." Andy asked, "And was he ever in trouble with the law?, and more importantly, Mike, have you ever been in trouble with the law?"

Mike looked away and was quiet. Eventually, he answered "Yes." Alice reacted visually by putting her hand over her face.

Obviously, this was information she wasn't aware of. Andy continued, "Did you serve time? If so, for what?"

At this point, Mike got up from the table, looked at Andy and said, "Go to hell!" and stormed out the front door.

Alice ran into her room and slammed the door. Andy looked at Greg, rolled his eyes, shook his head and said nothing.

Greg said, "I hope someday your daughter will be able to thank you for what you just did for her." Andy just sighed. He thanked Greg for his work and his time. He paid him. Greg left the house.

Andy knocked softly on Alice's door. He heard a muffled response and opened the door. She was lying on the bed with the covers over her head.

"Dad, I can't believe what just happened. I just can't believe it. He is, apparently, not the person I thought he was. I'm just sorry I had to find out like this." Andy replied, "I'm just glad you found it out now instead of after you married him."

Alice threw the covers off of her face, sat up and said, "You are so right about that….." She went over to Andy and gave him a hug, "Thank you!" She immediately slipped the ring off of her finger and placed it on her bedside table. "I think I'll mail this back to him. What a fool I have been."

Alice took a long hot shower and went to bed. She didn't receive any phone calls from Mike that evening. He knew he had been found out and that the engagement was off. He wasn't quite as clever as he thought he was.

Andy was busy realizing how on guard he still needed to be in protecting Alice, Joey, Mary and the farm. This was nearly as bad as having to deal with all of the Mid-Eastern crises he had faced. Would he ever be able to just relax?

Andy felt so badly for Alice and, at the same time, so grateful that he had seen Mike's car the day he did. They had been spared another bullet!

Aren't we all weary of having to discover yet one more person who isn't who they present themselves to be?

Unfortunately, manipulation is one of the greatest tools of mankind. We have mastered the craft.

It makes me think of words from the well-known psychologist, Carl Rogers who once said, "It never pays in the long run to present ourselves as someone we are not." Those are very wise words. Mike is yet another example of using that tool to deeply wound another person and make it that much harder to ever trust another man.

Our experiences change us. We are all impacted by the actions of one another, for good or for bad.

Alice's life has been quite traumatic. She saw her parents murdered. She lost her twin sister to COVID at age nine. She lost her adoptive mother, brother and sister. Now she has lost her fiancé. Her crooked path is largely about loss and trauma. Her strength lies with her veterinary skills. She can channel her energies into her strengths, just as Andy has had to do.

Sometimes life doesn't give us as many choices nor the specific choices we think we need in order to survive or to be happy. We need to be careful what we wish for. It's not always what is best for us. This is a life lesson for Alice. Her crooked path is unfolding in unforeseen ways. Her responses will continue to direct her path, whatever it might be.

How will these disclosures that came from Andy impact their relationship? Only time will tell.

Chapter Sixteen

Positive Manifestations

Over the next several months, Alice directed her energies into the equine project at the farm. They now had ten horses and could take in more programs for children. They were gaining a very positive reputation in the community. They were just beginning a program to allow people to come and rent the horses for a leader-led trail ride. Alice herself led most of those rides.

She was feeling very fulfilled from her work. She appeared to be adjusting in a healthy way to the breaking of her engagement.

She was moving on and it showed.

Joey was now a young man. He was enrolled in college courses on the internet. They were mostly veterinary courses. He was working hard to apply what he was learning to what he was doing. Andy, Mary and Alice all served as his mentors.

No longer was Mary's farm just a place that took in stray animals. It was becoming a world class equine therapy program for children. They were receiving applications from throughout the country, looking for a place to send traumatized children.

Mary and Andy were having to take a serious look at whether or not they wanted to begin such a program. It would take the farm in an entirely new direction. They would need to supply housing, food and therapists. It would be very costly but would likely support itself.

Andy and Mary were both doing critical research in order to come up with the best answer to the direction of the farm. Andy's experience as the CEO of the Foundation was invaluable in putting all of the pieces together.

Mary and Andy shared a very critical piece of this important puzzle. They both believed strongly in their mission to make a difference for good.

The next meeting attended by Mary, Andy, Alice and Joey was a very important one. After two hours of a lively discussion, they decided to vote on whether or not to take the next step to test the waters and the viability of taking on this huge project. The vote was unanimous.

The house was huge. They would hire a contractor to come in and carve out 2-3 more bedrooms and bathrooms. This would enable them to have six guests at a time. They really didn't want any more than that. They wanted to be certain that each troubled child would get the kind and amount of attention they deserved.

After taking care of their housing needs, the children would each need a 24/7 caretaker. Andy was very familiar with this critical need from his experiences at the Foundation. This would require a major advertising campaign. They would need to hire a major mental health person to oversee the clinical aspects of the program, likely a psychologist or psychiatrist.

They decided they all needed to set aside a block of time each week to discuss this project. They were all quite busy by now. They selected Sunday afternoons from 1-5 PM. They were very committed to building this program. The dye was cast.

The contractors were finished with the new construction to house the children. Next, they would need to select a start date and begin interviewing caretakers. This would be no small undertaking. Andy insisted he should be the one to manage this part of the project.

Mary and Alice were in charge of all of the equine issues necessary for the children. They would use the gentlest horses with very qualified equine guides. The children would be responsible for "their" horse all week. They would learn to saddle them, brush them, wash them, feed and water them. They would learn how to be a caretaker. This would be a great therapeutic tool and skill for each of them.

The team was starting to get very excited about the program. They all took a deep breath and placed the ads that they would be open to accept children for one week beginning in three months.

That marked the beginning of Summer.

All of the pieces were coming together, mostly because of Andy's previous experiences at the Foundation. In some ways, he was emulating policies and procedures he had learned at the Foundation. Much of it he had learned from his time with Allison. How great it would be if she were alive now to be part of this undertaking. She would be so excited to be part of it. Maybe she was already a part of it!

It was now one week before they would be open for business. They had hired two cooks, three maids, two handymen and a Board Certified Clinical Psychologist along with three therapists.

Since they had begun advertising, they had received more than 60 applications. It appeared, then, that they were already booked for several months. They would take six children at a time for one week each. They would arrive on Sunday and leave the following Saturday. Joey was put in charge of handling the schedules. He had developed and matured and seemed to be capable of handling that piece of the program. He seemed to take a lot of pride in being given the responsibility.

Everyone had their part to play in establishing a well-run program. Andy knew there would be bumps in the road they would need to problem-solve. He had no doubts they could handle them.

The children ranged in age from 10-16. Andy suggested they book the children according to their age in order to have children close to the same age each week. Joey did exactly as they asked. He presented a full schedule for the next few weeks.

For now, Andy was also handling the accounting issues. He had done it before and was comfortable with it. The cost for a week at the farm was $25,000. That was as low as they could go and still maintain the program.

This was kind of like being back at the Foundation for Andy.

He was using his same skill set. However, now, he was also using his animal skills. He was so pleased Alice was a full time employee there. He felt as though he was part of a family again. He felt beyond blessed that pieces of his life had come together again. He knew it was a strength greater than his that made it all possible.

It was Sunday. The children were arriving. The first group came from all parts of the USA. They were 10-11 year olds.

Each had their own set of traumatic issues. Their clinical files had been received and reviewed carefully before they were even accepted into the program. In fact, a few of the children were not assessed as being appropriate for their program and were not accepted.

Each child was shown to their room by their caretaker. They were each assisted in putting their personal belongings away.

They were then taken to the beautiful dining room where a table was set with a total variety of foods. It would be a week of smorgasbord foods. Each child was free to choose the foods they liked and would enjoy. There was plenty of everything.

Andy was surprised at how smoothly the week was going. It felt like clock work precision. Everyone was doing their jobs. The children seemed to be excited about taking care of their horse.

Andy spent time just observing everyone doing their jobs and he had such a deep level of gratitude for all the miracles that had occurred for such a program to ever have been created.

Isn't it interesting to observe how all of the pieces have been woven together to create this incredible healing opportunity for children.

It all started in a dilapidated building with a woman who cared about stray dogs. Then it received help from a man who also cared about animals who was able to support it.

Then it was a dream to find a piece of property that would be better suited to help the animals.

Then it was a miracle to find an unforeseen fortune inside of an old farmhouse.

Then it was ingenuity that allowed the miracle money to provide an even better facility to help animals.

Then it was the commitment and hard work of caring people to expand their love to more than one kind of animal.

Then it was the dream to bring all of the treasures and use it to help traumatized and hurting children.

A miracle has been created. It started with one woman's compassionate heart and her best efforts to do what she could. From there it all came together. No one gave up, no matter what! Perhaps that is the real and valuable secret here. Give what you can. Plant a seed and watch God water it!

Chapter Seventeen

A Sense of Gratitude

It was nearly time for the holidays. The new program had been in place for three months now. There had been no major problems. The team was amazed that things had all gone so well. They were very grateful. Everyone was working very hard. They were all tired, but it was a good tired. Now they all be able to enjoy six weeks off. It would be the time out everyone needed, including the animals.

There had been no incidents nor any resignations. The team was committed to making a difference for good. That was their motto. It was posted everywhere!

Alice had never seemed happier. Over time she could only be grateful for Andy's intervention in keeping her from making a huge mistake. It was a learning experience. She had moved on. She was actually dating a new guy now. He was also a veterinarian. Andy met him and took an instant liking to him. He was often at the house and part of supper. It was very comfortable for all of them. It was fun to talk about "animals" at dinner.

Mary couldn't be more proud of what the farm had become and the way it had developed. She knew she owed it all to Andy. He had been such a miracle in her life. If Kristy hadn't died he would never have returned to Seattle. We never really know how the circumstances of our lives will affect us. It had all worked out so well.

Joey had finished two years of college on the internet. He had actually located a local veterinary college where he could complete his last two years and still live there at the farm. It was exciting to all of them that he had decided to become a veterinarian. It was perfect. Again, Joey would never have come to the farm were it not for Andy. He was such an amazing man.

Andy was tired. He was greatly appreciative of the program they had created and operationalized. He actually saw some of the pieces of his life fitting together. It was a quiet realization for him. Sometimes he shared it with Kristy as he sat outside late at night looking at the water. He felt certain she was right there with him listening to every word. It made him smile just to think about it.

That Sunday afternoon as he and Alice and Bob were having dinner, Alice said that she and Bob had something to tell him.

She held out her hand to display a beautiful engagement ring. Andy took her hand and kissed it. He told her how happy he was for both of them.

Andy told them he was honored to know each of them and that he was grateful they were a part of his crooked path. That, too, was a miracle.

They wanted to be married there in the backyard of the house. They wanted a very simple ceremony. It was planned for Christmas Day!

This brought a huge smile from Andy. He said, "I'll bring the champagne." He got up from the table and hugged them both.

What a beautiful difference from the previous horrible interchange he and Alice had once experienced around the table. It felt like the end of the world for Alice. It wasn't. There was someone so much better suited for her right around the corner. Isn't it funny the way things just seem to work out sometimes.

Later that night, Andy found himself sitting outside by the water thinking about the events of the day. As he reflected on the wonderful changes in Alice's life, it caused him to do a serious reflection on the events of his own life.

Andy's earliest memory was of a very happy childhood with his mother and father. Their deaths in the plane crash sent him into a tailspin which eventually sent him to the Foundation. Due to no fault of his own, he was kidnapped and taken halfway around the world and shown a different way of life. Because of his kidnapper's greed, he was allowed to return to the USA. Because of his sainted grandfather, he was rescued and given a new life.

He would always remember his dog, Max, and the great comfort he had been to him. Eventually, he finished college at Stanford University

His grandfather passed away. He inherited more money than he could ever imagine. He married and had a son. His son was murdered. His wife divorced him and he attempted suicide.

Allison became his unseen angel, gave him a job and a place to live. More than that, she gave him hope. Then, he lost her.

Eventually, he met and married Kristy, one of the best decisions he ever made in his life. They adopted orphaned twin girls and lost one of them to COVID. Eventually they had a son and daughter of their own. They lost them both in a horrible accident. Eventually he lost his wife to cancer.

He and Alice moved back to Seattle and started a new life.

It led to events and programs they never could have foreseen before they came.

Their complex crooked paths were directed every step of the way. "He made a way in the wilderness that only He could see."

In short, Andy's life had been a complex weaving of little understood steps on a path where he usually could not see how he could possibly move forward. Sometimes, he couldn't even find the path. Nonetheless, the unseen angels always seemed to know the way. They still do.

Author's Conclusions

Like Andy, most of us are not able to see very far down our complex crooked path. In fact there may be long periods of our lives where we don't even see the path.

Sometimes, it's hard to believe there even is a path.

Sometimes it is just unimaginable that any loving Being would allow the path the world seems to be following.

Sometimes, we lose track of ourselves. We have days where we're not sure anymore of who we are, how we feel or if we even care about being on any path.

Sometimes we are so full of anxiety, fear, anger and depression that we could care less about having any concerns about a path.

Sometimes, we have what seems like a breakthrough moment when the path is crystal clear and we have a grateful heart to be on it.

Sometimes, we pray for a different path, a different life. We pray we can wake up and it will all be different, but that never happens. It challenges our strengths and our belief system.

Sometimes, we feel like cashing in our ticket. We may feel it's just not worth the stress anymore. We feel like giving up.

Eventually, like Andy, we come to understand that giving up is never an option.

CPSIA information can be obtained
at www.ICGtesting.com
Printed in the USA
BVHW062021011221
622865BV00006B/270

9 781638 716983